HISTORIC NEW YORK

A Tour of More Than 120 of the State's Top National Landmarks

Karen McLaughlin Cuccinello

Globe
Pequot

Guilford, Connecticut

Globe
Pequot

An imprint of The Rowman & Littlefield Publishing Group, Inc.
4501 Forbes Blvd., Ste. 200
Lanham, MD 20706
www.rowman.com

Distributed by NATIONAL BOOK NETWORK

British Library Cataloguing in Publication Information available

Library of Congress Cataloging-in-Publication Data

Names: Cuccinello, Karen, 1954- author.
Title: Historic New York : a tour of more than 120 of the state's top
   national landmarks / Karen McLaughlin Cuccinello.
Description: Guilford, Connecticut : Globe Pequot, [2021] | Series:
   Historic | Includes index.
Identifiers: LCCN 2021011529 | ISBN 9781493056378 (trade paperback) |
ISBN 9781493056385 (epub)
Subjects: LCSH: Historic sites—New York (State)—Guidebooks. |
   Memorials—New York (State)—Guidebooks. | New York (State)—Guidebooks.
Classification: LCC F120 .C83 2021 | DDC 917.4704/44—dc23
LC record available at https://lccn.loc.gov/2021011529

CONTENTS

CATSKILL MOUNTAINS

CENTRAL REGION

CHAUTAUQUA–ALLEGANY

FINGER LAKES

HUDSON VALLEY

LONG ISLAND

NEW YORK CITY

NIAGARA FRONTIER

THOUSAND ISLANDS

INTRODUCTION

History abounds in every nook and cranny of New York State (NYS). The state's natural attributes enticed people from all over the world to put down roots and make history here. The mountains invited trappers and loggers, the valleys lured farmers and merchants, the lakes put fish on the dinner table and vacationers on the shore, the Atlantic Ocean supported seafarers and ports, and rivers and canals provided water power and transportation. New York State, the eleventh state in the United States, ratified July 26, 1788, has a little bit of history everywhere.

My journey to discover the best historic sites in all sixty-two counties of NYS began in November 2019. The goal was to find two sites per county, offering as many different venues as possible. I believe I came up with a pretty good mix of sites that highlight air, rail, automobile, and water transportation, military, foods, women, religions, architecture, the arts, nature, indigenous Americans, and a plethora of some of the oldest and unique buildings that now house museums in NYS. Venues range in size from single small buildings to mansions to complexes.

The key to this journey was patience, persistence, and pliability. When I started researching sites, I first gleaned whatever information I could from their websites or Facebook pages (sometimes the Facebook pages have more up-to-date information). Then, in order to add additional information above and beyond online sources, I made contact via email; if no response I would then message through Facebook, and if still no response I would call. More often than not I would have to leave a message on the answering machine because their office hours usually depended on availability of volunteer staff. Some folks got back to me quickly and were very generous with descriptions of their sites, and some not so much. When receiving numerous emails from assorted agencies, I had to be careful to place information with the correct facility; at one point I had three Eriks, spelled the same way, emailing me at the same time. Some that I corresponded with were very accommodating and set up times to give me a special tour.

Previous to this project I had already visited about fifteen historic sites, which helped add information to those facilities. In order to add more particulars to the book, I visited as many sites as possible and ended up traveling to thirty sites in a ten-month period (thank goodness for my husband, Andy, who drove me to half of them). Since I started working on this book at about the time that some of the sites were shutting down for the winter, it was not always easy to make contact. Visiting the sites that were open was not always easy in the wintertime either, as I could not just decide to go somewhere next Tuesday when that day might choose to drop snow, sleet, or freezing rain. When I was in my thirties I might have still headed out in lousy weather, but now that I am in my sixties, no thank you, I'm not that daring anymore. Winter travel turned out to be the least of my problems when the coronavirus hit the United States.

All museums were closed by April 2020 due to the Covid-19 pandemic, and some sites remained closed for the rest of 2020, so research was a bit tricky during this time. All my visits to sites from July through September, when some reopened (usually on a limited basis), involved making appointments and wearing a mask on-site. But I muddled through and amazingly made my October 1 deadline for turning in my draft on time.

I met or corresponded with some very nice, dedicated historic site employees along my journey to uncover the secrets of their quest to preserve history. No matter how similar some of the sites may seem, they all have a uniqueness unlike any other. I hope that you enjoy the sites that I discovered and wish you safe travels when you are able to visit some of them. Try as I might, sometimes print quality photos were not obtainable for some of the sites.

Just a reminder: When you are visiting NYS, remember that we host all four often-fickle seasons here. A day in NYS, during any time of the year, can involve wearing a ski hat, jacket, pants, and boots in the morning and a baseball hat, T-shirt, shorts, and sandals in the afternoon. I know this as a fact, as I have lived in NYS my entire sixty-plus years.

ADIRONDACK MOUNTAINS

The Alice T. Miner Museum
9618 State Rte. 9, Chazy; (518) 846-7336; minermuseum.org; open May through Dec for guided tours; admission charged

The Alice, as it is often referred to, is considered to be a Colonial Revival museum, which would be enjoyable for all who are interested in the beginnings of America.

A Colonial Revival museum generally houses artifacts pertaining to the colonial period of America, which were usually collected between 1880 and 1930 by those interested in preserving the past. The Alice T. Miner Colonial Collection, as it was first named, was opened in 1924, by Alice, of course.

Alice Emma Trainer was born in 1863 in Goderich, Canada, then moved to Chicago, Illinois, with some of her siblings in the 1880s, where she met and married William "Will" Henry Miner in 1895. Will's uncle had left him his 144-acre farm in Chazy, New York, in 1893, so they started spending time in Chazy after their marriage. Will bought an adjacent farm in 1902, and in 1903 he and Alice started to renovate the farmhouse that would come to be named Heart's Delight Cottage.

Will Miner made his fortune while in Chicago as an entrepreneur and railroad industrialist. His philanthropic endeavors in Chazy included the Chazy Central Rural School and the Physician's Hospital, and he oversaw construction of hydroelectric dams and powerhouses. Will and Alice's farm grew to fifteen thousand acres of land, which eventually required eight hundred employees to operate. Following his death the William H. Agricultural Research Institute was established, also in Chazy.

Alice opened her first museum of ceramics in 1915 in Harmony Hall, which was a guest house on their Heart's Delight Farm. While Alice was organizing this little museum, she realized she needed a bigger building for her collection, so her husband bought what was referred to as the Old Stone Store in the Village of Chazy in 1916. The Old Stone Store was razed and the museum, fashioned as the colonial home you see today, was built using some of the Old Stone Store blocks between 1924 and 1926. Following Will's death in 1930, Alice put all her efforts into her museum and other philanthropic endeavors in Chazy until her death in 1950.

The Alice holds furniture, decorative arts, and artifacts from around the world. "This museum is unique in that it is essentially a time capsule of what Alice T. Miner collected in the early part of the twentieth century. It started as Alice's vision of what an early American home might have been like, and the museum staff have tried to remain true to that while providing the context that helps explain her choices," says the museum director.

The furniture ranges from simple Windsor rockers to a high-style Queen Anne chest. Alice was not one to stick to a particular style or period of furniture.

The third-floor ballroom houses six hundred pieces of ceramics and glass. Most of the pieces in the collection are of English and French origin from the late eighteenth through nineteenth centuries.

The baskets in the collection are Klickitat, Hupa, and Yurok-Karok in origin, made in California, Oregon, and Washington State. The baskets are scattered around the museum along with a number of other Native American artifacts.

The textile collection includes quilts, coverlets, samplers, rugs, and other textiles produced by early American women. Not only are the finished products displayed, the implements that made them such as spinning wheels, carding combs, and pincushions are also on display.

The book and manuscript collection is impressive in its diversity. There is a Bible dated 1526 and novels into the early twentieth century. The manuscripts include letters written by Marquis de Lafayette and poets such as Henry Wadsworth Longfellow.

The Alice also houses a wide assortment of artifacts that do not fit into any particular category, such as clocks, coins, and armaments. "When the museum received President Lincoln's White House foot bath, Alice thought it was meant to hold ice and chill a bottle of wine," says the program coordinator.

There is also an archive of ephemera that researchers can utilize by appointment. Call before you visit Alice's eclectic collection to find out tour times.

War of 1812 and Plattsburgh Air Force Base Museums
31 Washington Rd., Plattsburgh; (518) 566-1814;
battleofplattsburgh.org and plattsburghafbmuseum.org;
open May through Oct; admission by donation

One site with two museums, only four hundred feet apart, offers insight into the activities of the US military spanning the years 1812 to 1995.

The museums, which are owned and operated by the Battle of Plattsburgh Association, delve into the entire War of 1812, with emphasis on the battles in Plattsburgh and the many ways the military utilized what would become the Plattsburgh Air Force Base (PAFB).

The War of 1812 formally began when President James Madison declared war on Great Britain on June 18, 1812. War was declared due to assorted political and economic conflicts, and naval blockades were put in place by the UK to prevent the United States from selling goods to France. This was a bold move considering that America was only thirty-six years old in 1812 and Madison was only our fourth president. The victories at Plattsburgh helped bring about the end of the war, which was officially declared on February 17, 1815.

The PAFB was then used for numerous reasons by different branches of the US military. The camp was turned over to the US Army Air Force in 1945. PAFB was the home of the Strategic Air Command from 1954 to 1992 and the Air Mobility Command from 1992 to 1995. Strategic Air Command was both a US Department of Defense Specified Command and a US Air Force Major Command, responsible for Cold War command and control of two of the three components of the US military's strategic nuclear strike forces. The mission of Air Mobility Command is to provide rapid, global mobility and support for America's armed forces. The featured exhibit at the PAFB Museum is "The Trainer," which is nearly identical to the cockpit of an FB-111A. Check out all the dials and knobs while you sit in "The Trainer."

The War of 1812 Museum houses a small theater, an interpretive center, exhibit space, and an art gallery.

The interpretive center chronicles the events of the battles at Plattsburgh within the context of the entire war. A five-by-fifteen-foot interactive battlefield diorama gives an aerial view of the thirty-thousand-acre battlefield. Through the diorama visitors can visualize the movements of the forces throughout the Village of Plattsburgh, the surrounding countryside, and on the waters of the Cumberland Bay. Throughout the center are scale models of some of the American vessels that fought in naval battles and displays depicting battles and soldiers.

There is an exhibit that commemorates the Plattsburgh Veteran Exempts and the Chesterfield Silver Grays. These units were organized during the War of 1812 by local Revolutionary War veterans, who supplied their own weapons and helped the US forces.

In 1812, Zebulon Pike (of Pike's Peak fame) was sent to Plattsburgh to winter three regiments of troops in the subzero forest southwest of the village. Pike's Cantonment, one of Pike's cabins, has been built inside the museum and houses some of the artifacts from the original campsite.

If you like paintings, visit the gallery dedicated to original works of art relating to the battles at Plattsburgh and the War of 1812. The oil painting that leads to the entrance of the art gallery, called the Battle of Lake Champlain, was painted in 1884 by Julian O. Davidson.

In the Press-Republican Theater, named after a local newspaper, a short documentary titled *The Battles of Plattsburgh* can be viewed, or you might catch one of their special presentations.

Finish your visit to the War of 1812 Museum with a trip to the gift shop, which is filled with historical books and memorabilia.

Fort Ticonderoga
102 Fort Ti Rd., Ticonderoga; (518) 585-2821; fortticonderoga.org; open May through Oct plus special winter events; admission charged

You might think that Fort Ticonderoga is just a military museum, but it is also a complex of assorted venues and is wonderful for all ages.

I visited this site with my family a few years ago. Our group consisted of some sixty-year-olds, thirty-year-olds, and, at the time of the visit, three boys ages four,

nine, and fourteen, and we all found something of interest, even the teenager. He was enthralled by the way they cooked food in an oven built into a mound of dirt. The younger boys loved the musket firing demonstration.

Fort Ticonderoga was originally named Fort Carillon and was built by the French between 1755 and 1757 during the French and Indian War. Not long after the completion of the fort, the British gained and kept control until the American Revolution. The American Continental Army controlled the fort from 1775 to 1777, then it went back to the British until 1781 when they abandoned it. The fort fell into disrepair until it came into the hands of the Pell family in about 1820. The Pells restored the fort through the years, then opened it to the public in 1909. The Fort Ticonderoga Association now oversees the fort.

"The Artillery Laboratory" offers examples of artillery attire and "A Ticonderoga Chronology" explores the history of the Ticonderoga peninsula. "Bullets & Blades: The Weapons of America's Colonial Wars and Revolution" offers a world-renowned collection of weaponry. The "Sarah Pell's Struggle for History and Human Rights" exhibit offers insight into Mrs. Sarah Gibbs (Thompson) Pell's (1878–1939) role in preserving the fort and securing women's rights. "Potter, Pork & Pigeon: Fort Ticonderoga's 18th-Century Menu" offers displays of eating utensils and dishes used by eighteenth-century soldiers. "Object Lessons: Perspectives on Material Culture" explores objects from the fort from the perspective of function, manufacturing, art, and culture. "Diorama-Rama: History in Miniature" reconstructs the past in miniature. "Ticonderoga, A Legacy" chronicles the legacy of Ticonderoga through the military and popular culture from the eighteenth century though the 2000s. "Iron and Stone: Building Fort Carillon" examines the construction of Fort Carillon through techniques and tools. "Sickness, Injury & Medicine" highlights what armies of the eighteenth century knew about medicine. "Art of Resistance: Selections from the Robert N. Nittolo Collection" highlights the pivotal Native American role in the wars.

Numerous tours are offered with titles such as Key to the Continent, Fort Ticonderoga Museum, Breaking Ground, Mount Defiance: Witness to History, and a scenic boat tour on Lake Champlain.

Living-history demonstrations might include weapons demonstrations, a soldiers' dinner, tailoring, shoemaking, maritime trades, carpentry, livestock, fife and drums, and musket maintenance.

Hands-on-activities, geared toward children, might include helping soldiers with their daily duties, making a historical hat, or discovering the science and math behind maritime trades.

Outdoor activities that are within walking distance of the fort proper are King's Garden, Mount Defiance, Carillon Battlefield, and the Corn Maze (in season). Visitors of King's Garden can enjoy the fort's six-acre garden and smell the fragrant heritage flowers. Mount Defiance offers a bird's-eye view of Ticonderoga's military landscape. You can hike or drive up the mountain and eat a picnic lunch in the pavilion there as well.

Carillon Battlefield offers a hike that is a 1.7-mile loop through the area where the Battle of Carillon took place on July 8, 1758. This was considered to be the bloodiest battle in North American history until the Civil War. The Heroic Corn Maze has a Kiddie Maze and a "Captain A Ship" Maze Quest that's a type of scavenger hunt as well.

"The fort debuts a new chapter in its story each year through historical interpretation and major museum exhibits, making it an annual tourist and family destination with new adventures every year," says the group tour and communications coordinator.

As you can see, Fort Ticonderoga is much, much more than a fort.

Lake Placid Olympic Museum
2634 Main St., Lake Placid; (518) 302-5326; lpom.org;
open year-round; admission charged

This museum is the only official Olympic Games museum in the United States; perfect for the winter sports enthusiast and interesting for all ages to learn about this piece of America's history.

The first summer Olympics occurred in Greece in 1896, the first winter Olympics took place in France in 1924, the first winter Olympics in North America was in Lake Placid February 4–15, 1932, and the 1980 winter Olympics were back in Lake Placid February 13–24. Lake Placid is one of only six sites to host the winter Olympics two times. The 1932 games hosted seventeen nations and the 1980 games had thirty-seven nations.

Philip G. Wolff, a bobsled driver, was the founder of the museum. His goal was to promote the Olympic movement through programs, education, and exhibits.

The "Quest for Speed" exhibit explores the life of a speed skater. There is a timeline showcasing the design evolution of speed skating equipment, along with interactive activities and graphic text panels. Some of the Olympic athletes highlighted are Charles Jewtraw, Jack Shea, Valentine Bialas, Jeanne Ashworth, Bonnie Blair, Apolo Ohno, and Eric Heiden. The collection includes the first Winter Olympic medal ever awarded for the five-hundred-meter speed skating competition, which was won by Lake Placid native Charles Jewtraw in the 1924 Games in Chamonix, France.

The "Ski Jumping History" exhibit gives an overview of the sport in the early years when skiing meant cross-country touring and ski jumping. Lake Placid had a ski jump before ski jumping was first included in the Olympics in 1924.

The "Sonja Henie: Perfection on Ice" exhibit features Norwegian Olympian Sonja Henie (1912–1969), one of the greatest figure skaters of all times. She competed in the first Olympic Winter Games in 1924 at age eleven, where she finished last, but in the next three Olympics she won gold medals. Sonja's passion for perfection changed the world of figure skating; she was the first to captivate an audience with her beauty, costumes, and athleticism. She also helped transform figure skating into an entertainment sport.

The "Miracle on Ice" exhibit offers original footage of the game played between the US hockey team and the Soviet Union (USSR) in 1980. The amateur US team beat the world-class Soviet Union team 4–3, then went on to the final round and beat Finland 4–2 to win the gold medal. Some refer to the game against the Soviet Union as the "greatest sports moment" of the twentieth century. Equipment and other artifacts are also included in this exhibit. I do remember watching some of this game; it was an exhilarating moment in time.

The "1932 Olympics" exhibit explains how the Village of Lake Placid won the bid for the 1932 Olympics and offers memorabilia from the Games, and the equipment used at the time by speed skaters, hockey players, and bobsledders. It is pretty amazing that the 1932 Olympics took place in the midst of the Great Depression.

The "Curling" exhibit explores the strategy and history behind this unique Olympic event that started as a demonstration sport in 1932. You can practice your skills against your friends here.

The "Olympic and Parade Uniforms" exhibit shows the emergence of brand names in the fashion industry in the 1980 Olympic uniforms, and the uniforms that Lake Placid "hometown heroes" wore marching in the opening ceremony parades. Lake Placid has sent at least one athlete to every Olympic Winter Games since 1924.

The "Sliding Sports" exhibit describes the history of bobsled, skeleton, and luge with a collection of sleds, photographs, and sliding sports equipment. Bobsled races were included in the 1924 Olympics, skeleton in 1928, and luge came on the scene in 1964.

"Foretelling the Future: The National Weather Service at the 1980 Olympic Winter Games" features what the meteorologists did, equipment that was used, and photos from the 1980 Olympics.

The museum archives hold an extensive collection of Olympic materials, which include both final reports and result books from Winter Olympiads along with Olympic Winter Sports Reference Books. Collections also include photographs from the III Olympic Winter Games in 1932 and the 1980 Olympic Winter Games. The archives are open to researchers.

The Olympic Museum is located in the Olympic Center, which is only a few feet from the Herb Brooks Arena where the 1980 "Miracle on Ice" hockey game took place and the Jack Shea Arena, home of the first indoor Winter Olympics skating arena.

"Many visitors have no idea that Lake Placid hosted two Olympics and that the Athlete's Village in 1980 became a federal correctional institute," says the museum director.

If you get hungry following your visit, there is a cafeteria on the upper level of the Olympic Center, where you can enjoy breakfast or lunch overlooking the Speed Skating Oval.

Franklin County Historical & Museum Society
51 Milwaukee St., Malone; (518) 483-2750; franklinhistory.org; open June through Sept; admission charged

The House of History, as the museum is called, is a smaller museum all about preserving and presenting the history of Franklin County, with emphasis on William Almon Wheeler, the nineteenth vice president.

The museum is in a Tuscan-style brick home that was built by Nathan Knapp in 1864. There were a few owners before George W. Crooks bought it in 1895, and his daughter Elizabeth (Crooks) Kirk lived there until her death in 1973. Elizabeth was married to F. Roy Kirk (1877–1921), a Malone businessman and the founder of Purity Ice Cream.

The museum houses a unique collection of original furnishings and belongings of Franklin County's own William Almon Wheeler, US vice president from 1877 to 1881. William was born in 1819 in Malone and died in 1887 in Malone. He was also an attorney and politician representing NYS during the 1860s and 1870s.

Period rooms showcase the mid to late 1800s time period and include the Wheeler bedroom, dining room, and kitchen with woodstove, and a country store that also doubles as a gift shop.

A longtime volunteer at the museum told me that visitors are often very interested in their diorama of the Saint Regis Mohawk Indian Reservation set in the eighteenth century. It is also known by its Mohawk name, Akwesasne.

A couple of poignant artifacts are two framed letters that were both mailed from Washington, DC, and sent to Malone. The first letter was written by William Wheeler's wife, Mary (King) Wheeler, shortly before her death in March 1876 and a year before William took office as vice president. The second letter is written by William pertaining to his sadness following his wife's death.

The Schryer Center for historical and genealogical research, located in the Carriage House behind the museum, houses Franklin County archival materials and family histories useful for local or family research. The center is open year-round; call ahead for hours.

The Almanzo Wilder Homestead
177 Stacy Rd., Malone; (518) 483-1207; almanzowilderfarm.com;
open Memorial Day weekend through Sept; admission charged

This is the site of the original home of Almanzo Wilder; perfect for families who enjoy visiting life in northern New York during the mid-nineteenth century and the *Little House on the Prairie* books written by his wife, Laura Ingalls. No other property is visible from the 84 acre Wilder Homestead so you have a feeling of serenity much like it was in the 1800s.

Almanzo's father, James, who was originally from Vermont, purchased the property in 1840, then cleared the land and built the buildings. Almanzo (1857–1949) was one of six children born to James Mason and Angelina (Day) Wilder. In the 1870 census report for the town of Burke, James is a fifty-eight-year-old farmer, Angelina is forty-nine and keeping house, Laura Ann is twenty-four and a schoolteacher, Royal G. is twenty-one and works on the farm, Eliza Jane is an eighteen-year-old schoolteacher, Alice M. is sixteen, Almanzo is twelve, Perley is one. Remember, Eliza Jane and Perley were characters on some of the episodes of the *Little House on the Prairie* TV show.

The museum is located within the visitor center and is home to a collection of period artifacts, farm tools, photos, replica homestead models, and information pertaining to the Wilder and Ingalls families, and farm life. Interpretation of this site is based on the book, *Farmer Boy*, which Almanzo's wife, Laura, wrote in 1933. *Farmer Boy* recounts Almanzo's life in the year 1866 when he was nine years old.

rick auger photo

The other buildings in the complex are the post and beam–constructed Wilder farmhouse, barns, pump house, hen house, and one-room schoolhouse. Some of the household artifacts in the Wilder home were discovered on the property during archaeological digs. "This is the only house that Laura Ingalls Wilder wrote about in her children's books that still stands on its existing foundation," says a board member.

Kitchen gardens, near the barns, were reconstructed using plans that Almanzo drew for Laura. The original foundations of the side barns were discovered during the archaeological digs, and some of the stones were used for the foundations of the reconstructed Big Barn and South Barn.

The complex also includes a research library, gift shop, and nature trail to the Wilder family frontage on the Trout River.

There are many other museums across the country pertaining to the Wilder and Ingalls families. "On display in the Wilder home is one half of a coverlet woven in linsey-woolsey by Almanzo's mother, Angelina (Day) Wilder. It was divided by the descendants of Almanzo's brother Perley, and the other half is displayed by the Laura Ingalls Wilder Memorial Society in DeSmet, South Dakota," says a board member.

Fulton County Museum
237 Kingsboro Ave., Gloversville; (518) 725-2203; fultoncountyhistoricalsociety.org; open Memorial Day through Columbus Day; admission free, donations appreciated

This museum truly has something for everyone pertaining to Fulton County, and artifacts are literally stretched from floor to ceiling in all ten rooms. Something you want to be sure and see is the largest glove in the world (fifty-seven inches by thirty inches), and the smallest gloves (about two inches long) are on display as well.

The museum opened in 1973 in the old Kingsboro School building, which was built in 1900 on the site of the Kingsboro Academy. Permanent exhibits explore the community's educational history, glove and leather heritage, military service, civic organizations, businesses, the Fonda, Johnstown & Gloversville Railroad, and sports history. Artifacts are well marked. Every room covers different topics in no particular order, so where you start is your choice.

The Sports room houses an assortment of baseball uniforms and related paraphernalia. The team with the most recognition was the Gloversville-Johnstown minor league team, in operation from 1937 to 1951.

The Military room is packed with artifacts from the 1700s to the current time, including firearms, swords, uniforms, and a Native American longhouse. My favorite was a section dedicated to women who served with their uniforms,

photos, and mini bios. "The military room is often a favorite of visitors," says the museum director.

The School area is filled with yearbooks, photographs, uniforms, and trophies.

The Technology room is chock-full of radios, televisions, cameras, typewriters, adding machines, and record players that span multiple centuries.

The Tanning and Glove room is a favorite for visitors, as gloves and Gloversville are synonymous. There are tools of the tanning process with a representation of an actual glove shop. Between 1880 and 1950 Gloversville is said to have produced 90 percent of the gloves sold in the United States. Every type of glove imaginable is on display. I liked the tiniest ones, which were used for advertising, the best. The director told me that some visitors make a beeline straight to the glove room.

The Weaving, Spinning and Victorian room is full of quilts, looms, and a huge spinning wheel.

The Public Service room has artifacts related to police and fire departments, nursing service, and a pharmacy display. This room also includes a jail cell from 1913, a gallows, a traffic light, and a working fire alarm system. The hangman's noose/gallows was used for the last time in Fulton County on January 24, 1846, to hang Elizabeth Van Valkenburgh, age forty-six, who murdered her husband, John, on March 18, 1845, by putting arsenic in his beverage. In a confession

to this murder, she also confessed to killing her first husband, in 1833, in the same manner.

The Railroad and Farming room houses antique farming implements, artifacts from the 1902 Mountain Lake Railroad wreck site, and a model train layout. The Fonda, Johnstown & Gloversville (FJ&G) Railroad was in operation from 1870 to 1974, then operated as the Delaware & Otsego Railroad for ten more years.

Several paranormal investigations have taken place at the museum. The observations made by the investigators are available for review.

Fulton County's history is well represented at the Fulton County Museum.

Johnson Hall State Historic Site
139 Hall Ave., Johnstown; (518) 762-8712; parks.ny.gov/historic-sites/johnsonhall/; open May through Oct; admission charged

This is an elegant, polished two-story (three stories with the basement) museum that highlights the opulence of the original owner via guided tours.

Johnson Hall is an English Georgian–style home built in 1763 on the estate of Irish immigrant Sir William Johnson (1715–1774) and Molly Brant, a Mohawk Indian, and their eight children. William was the first baronet of New York, a title bestowed on him in 1755 by the British Crown, and the next year he was appointed superintendent of Indian Affairs. Previous to Molly he had three children with Catherine Weisenberg (ca. 1723–1759) and potentially had relations with other Brant women. Johnson was the largest single landowner and

most influential individual in the colonial Mohawk Valley. Following William's death his eldest son became John Johnson, a Loyalist, took over the estate and the title of baronet for a short time, then left for Canada. Johnson Hall was a private residence until 1906 when NYS purchased it.

An eye-catching part of the mansion is the huge front and back doors, over four feet wide and about a foot taller than the average door, which were locked with a very large skeleton key. To the left of the mansion is the West Stonehouse, also part of the guided tour, which housed slaves who ran the farm before 1827. There is a fireplace in the middle of the Stonehouse, time period mattresses, and a list of articles kept in the "Negro" room, from back in the day, on the table. The other outbuilding, to the right, is a reproduction of a time period building that houses a couple of displays and a small gift shop.

On the first floor of the mansion is a dining room that often fed ten to thirty visitors, a social gathering/dining area, and the children's and parents' bedrooms. Home life and business life were intermingled, with visitors on a daily basis from various Indian tribes and immigrants to the area. All but the children's bedroom displays portraits of the Johnson family. Upstairs had the same size center hallway as the first floor and four guest bedrooms that could also double as meeting rooms.

During my tour here I saw three artifacts that I have never seen before. There were about a dozen black buckets about eighteen inches high with a ten-inch opening at the top in the large center entrance hall. I thought they were for horse feed, but they were for water in the summer, or sand in the winter, to

put out potential fires. Another unusual artifact was a punch bowl with notches around the edge to hold the stem of wine glasses so that the glasses could be chilled on ice. The final surprise was a buffalo hide, fur side down, with a painting on it, on an upstairs bed.

My tour guide gave a thorough overview of the furnishings, inhabitants, and visitors of Johnson Hall.

Adirondack Experience, the Museum on Blue Mountain Lake
9097 State Rte. 30, Blue Mountain Lake; (518) 352-7311; theadkx.org; open May through Oct; admission charged

This is truly an oasis in the middle of a forest that offers a history of life in the Adirondacks through a variety of mediums and is perfect for all ages. Families might like to pick up the scavenger hunt at the visitor center to add a little more adventure to the day.

I have been to this site twice in the past: once with grandsons and once without. It was a great experience either way but more fun to go with children, especially to see their excitement upon finding something they could touch or operate. They particularly liked climbing up the Whiteface Fire Tower. Besides being fun for the kids, the fire tower offers a spectacular view that adults will appreciate, probably more than the kids.

Daily activities that occur different times of the day include feeding the fish at Marion River Carry Pavilion, demonstrations of Adirondack boatbuilding by the

boatbuilder-in-residence, and Native American artisans-in-residence demonstrating their crafts in the "Life in the Adirondacks" exhibit area.

The museum features historic buildings with exhibits: The Reising Schoolhouse, built in 1907, offers family activities such as games, toys, and crafts from a bygone era; Artist's Cottage was used as a summer house by landscape painter Gustave Wiegand and is furnished with rustic furniture; Sunset Cottage is a one-room cabin from Camp Cedars on Forked Lake, decorated with split-spruce pole siding; Marion River Carry Pavilion is home to demonstrations and activities as well as a 1901 H. K. Porter Company steam engine and passenger car (my grandsons liked the train a lot); and the Kids Cabin and Old-Fashioned Washroom allows children to pump water from the well, scrub cloths on a washboard, and hang them to dry.

Permanent exhibits are "The Buck Lake Club," an Adirondack twentieth-century one-room log cabin hunting camp, and "Life in the Adirondacks," a building that offers an interactive exploration of the Adirondack Park and its people. First stop by the Wilderness Stories Introduction Theater and view a video about the beauty of the Adirondacks, then move on to the five galleries that explore different aspects of the Adirondacks.

The "Call of the Wilderness" gallery explores a variety of people, through videos, who were drawn to the Adirondacks, such as Teddy Roosevelt. The exhibit also brings to life the private railroad station and Pullman car with audio soundscapes. "A Peopled Wilderness" explores the story of the Mohawk and Abenaki cultures

through artifacts, video interviews, music, and a language learning station. This gallery also includes an example of a traditional campsite once used by the indigenous people. The "Roughing It" area explores ways that people lived in the Adirondacks, either seasonally or permanently. The log cabin of Anne LaBastille, an author and naturalist who championed the pioneering life for women, is on display. "Adirondack Tough: Working in the Wilderness" reviews outdoor occupations, in particular the mining industry. There is an interactive activity of breaking up a log jam that allows visitors to experience firsthand how treacherous it was to be an Adirondack lumberjack in the late nineteenth century. "Our Adirondack Park" explores the many different perspectives of people who live, work, and visit here today. "Boats and Boating in the Adirondacks" has a large collection of authentic guide boats and canoes, and illustrates the importance of boats for transportation and leisure. The Log Hotel, built in 1876, includes the exhibit "Hotels, Camps and Clubs," featuring artifacts related to travel, lodging, and summer camps in the Adirondacks.

A couple of areas have revolving exhibits so that there is something new to see every year. The museum also offers some Cabin Fever Sundays during the winter. Cabin Fever Sunday presentations include a wide-ranging look at life in the Adirondacks.

A new experience is the Minnow Pond Trail and Boathouse. Take the three-quarter-mile easy stroll to Minnow Pond just for the fun of a hike, and rent a boat, for extended fun, at the boathouse. This activity might have weather limitations.

After you finish your day of exploring the Adirondack Experience, stop by the extensive gift shop and/or Lake View Cafe.

Piseco Lake Historical Society's Riley House & Riley Tavern

155 Old Piseco Rd., Piseco; gluseum.com; open July and Aug; admission free, donations welcome

Small in physical size but big in history and unique in that the tavern is the last surviving tavern/saloon in the Adirondacks.

The tavern got its name from Hugh Riley, a bachelor, originally from Ireland. Information from the town of Arietta (Piseco is within Arietta) census reports lists a few different birth years for Hugh between 1850 and 1857, and his arrival in the United States listed a few different dates also, but I think he arrived during the 1870s. There is record of him purchasing the building in 1887, and the 1892 census states he was an innkeeper. Following Hugh's death in 1939, his niece Mrs. Mary Ellen Donahue was bequeathed his property.

Molly K. Rockwell, a real estate broker, bought Hugh's home and saloon in 1954 and turned the saloon into a museum a few years later. During the renovations the cellar started to crumble, so Molly had the building moved within spittoon-hitting distance of the original site. Newspaper articles about Molly's purchase stated the original name was the old Rudeston Saloon (Rudeston was an old name for a hamlet in Arietta), which also housed the post office in 1909. Rockwell willed the house and tavern to the Town of Arietta with the stipulation that they would be used as a historical museum, and in 1986 the Piseco Lake Historical Society was formed.

The Riley House was built during the mid-1800s and was a boardinghouse for tannery workers and a hotel. The tavern was built during the 1880s, and besides the bar it had a trapdoor, a secret back room for gambling, and a room upstairs for sleeping quarters.

The museum buildings have a number of different exhibits pertaining to local history involving hotels, World War I and II, the Civil War, town basketball and baseball teams, the lumbering industry, ice cutting, beaches, nineteenth-century travel to Piseco, boating, and more.

"Visitors greatly enjoy seeing the tavern with its original 1880s cherry bar, and some guests have even taken measurements of the bar with photographs to reproduce it in their own homes," says the museum president.

In the main house, the display featuring local hermit Foxey Brown is always of interest. Foxey Brown, a hunting guide, was involved in the disappearance of Carlton Banker, the Cayadutta superintendent of the electric division Fonda, Johnstown & Gloversville Railroad, in November 1916, and there is still a mystery lingering as to what happened. Banker was on a hunting trip with a few other men, and Foxey was supposedly the last person to see him alive. The skeletal remains of Banker were discovered four years later, in November 1922, by Spruce Lake, but Foxey Brown had disappeared from the Adirondacks by that time, so there are still no answers for his demise.

Erie Canal Cruises

800 Mohawk St., Herkimer; (315) 717-0350; eriecanalcruises.com; open May through Oct; admission charged

This landmark offers a scenic boat ride and a history lesson all rolled up into one—enjoyable for all ages.

The digging of the Erie Canal began 1817 in Utica and was completed in 1825. It traversed 363 miles and included eighty-three locks that would raise and lower boats through sections with different water levels. During construction the canal was often called "Clinton's Folly" or "Clinton's Ditch," named after the NYS governor at the time, Dewitt Clinton, because people thought it was a waste of money. But of course it ended up helping NYS to grow immensely. This cruise takes you through Lock #18, at Jacksonburg, which is one of thirty-five locks still in operation.

The company offers Erie Canal daily Sightseeing Cruises, Friday Night Party Cruises, and Living History Cruises on their *Lil' Diamond II* or *III* tour boats. The cruises start and finish at the dock by the Gems Along the Mohawk gift shop and restaurant.

"A significant aspect about our site is that it is one of the most historically intact sections of the Erie Canal. You can clearly see the original 1828 Erie Canal, the original towpath that the mules used to pull the boats from, and the current-day Erie Canal all side by side near Lock 18. With the new Empire State Trail on the original towpath, this cross section encompasses over two hundred years of transportation innovation in New York State! Along your journey you might also see any number of vessels, from fabulous yachts to kayaks," says the marketing director.

The Sightseeing Cruise, daytime or evening, is a ninety-minute narrated journey involving the history of the construction of the canal and the landmarks along the way. You will go by Fort Herkimer Church, one of the oldest churches in NYS, and

catch glimpses of local birds in the Plantation Island Wildlife Management Area. Then you will be raised and lowered twenty feet in Lock #18, one of the last remaining locks operating with one-hundred-plus-year-old equipment, and head back to Herkimer. I went on this cruise a few years ago and found it quite informative; watching the way the lock operates is a unique and unforgettable experience.

Friday Night Parties are themed cruises that offer entertainment, dancing, a full bar, and munchies, so this would be an adult event.

The Living History Cruise is a six-hour event that buses you to the historic home of Revolutionary War hero General Nicholas Herkimer. Upon arrival you will tour the general's mansion, enjoy a barbecue, and watch a chocolate-making demonstration, then board a *Lil' Diamond* vessel and go through locks #17 and #18 back to Gems Along the Mohawk.

A few years ago, I had occasion to see a drained lock because I followed the activities involved in hauling half of a new lock gate. My husband Andy was the truck driver bringing it out to lock #27 in Lyons, New York. The lock gate he hauled was made in Schenectady and was twenty-eight feet wide (mind you, that's only half a gate). It was moved mostly on highways and at night with numerous police and escort cars. Traffic could not pass the load because it filled both lanes. It was a huge endeavor that involved numerous agencies to move the gate about one hundred miles. The lock gate was replacing a gate that had been in operation for one hundred years.

There are two gates/doors on either side of a lock that open and close to let water in to raise a boat to the next level of the canal and then open up the other side to let the boat out. It's hard to explain; you just have to see it to believe it.

Russian History Foundation
**1407 Robinson Rd., Jordanville; (315) 858-2468;
russianhistoryfoundation.org; open year-round; admission charged**

There are only a handful of museums around the United States that offer Russian artifacts. This unique smaller museum is located on the grounds of the Holy Trinity Monastery and is geared toward an adult audience. While on monastery grounds, kindly show respect for their religious beliefs. This museum collection is beautifully presented in display cases, organized by time period, with detailed descriptions. Items include Russian church artifacts, military collectibles, cultural and religious art, and antiques that date back, in some cases, over a thousand years. Among these are a substantial number of objects that belonged to the Russian Imperial family, many having been donated by members of the Romanov family.

An especially significant set of imperial provenance artifacts are the nearly ninety objects belonging to Tsar Nicholas II, members of his family, and their attendants,

which were collected as material evidence by investigator Nikolai Sokolov after the royal family's murder in July 1918 in Yekaterinburg.

Nicholas/Nikolai Alexandrovish Romanov (1868–1918) was the last emperor of Russia. He married Alexandra Feodorovna in 1894, and they had four daughters and a son.

Other unique and rare items in the museum collection are the medals, orders, and banners of various anti-Bolshevik military forces from the time of the Russian Civil War.

Interesting items I saw during my visit included an Easter egg with icon of Descent into Hades, Moscow late eighteenth century; icons of Christ Pantocrator and Kazan, Mother of God, Moscow 1896 to 1908; Greatmartyr and Healer Panteleimon, Moscow late nineteenth century; four Hierarchs of Moscow, late seventeenth to early eighteenth century; pendant icon of Christ Moscow, "Georgian" Mother of God icon, Moscow mid-eighteenth century; chalice, Moscow 1806; plashchanitsa (shroud), Moscow late nineteenth century; bishop's sakkos (a liturgical vestment worn by bishops), nineteenth century; embroidered palitsa (palitsa or epigonationis is a component of the vestments), Russia nineteenth century; amethyst panagia, late nineteenth century, and panagia with icon of Christ, Moscow 1829 (panagia means "The All-Holy"); Metropolitan Anthony's mitre (mitre is headgear worn by bishops), early twentieth century; cuffs, beginning of twentieth century; Order of Saint George IV Class, early twentieth century; Saint Nicholas the Wonderworker, Russia late nineteenth century; music for the twelve great feasts, Russia 1825 to 1850; Feeding Horn 1871; baptismal crosses and icon pendants, late eighteenth to early twentieth centuries; icon of the Old Testament Trinity, late nineteenth century; Easter egg with Fischbeck Displaced Persons "DP" Camp, 1949, and Soviet propaganda plates, 1920 to 1922.

The favorite artifact of the seminary student who escorted me into the museum was the carved figure of Saint Nil Stolobensky, because carved figures are rare. My favorite was a St. Petersburg baptismal gown, circa 1858, worn by Grand Duke Konstantin Konstantinovish Romanov (1858–1915), grandson of Nicholas I.

It is possible to tour the Holy Trinity Monastery, founded in 1930, which is under the jurisdiction of the Russian Orthodox Church Outside Russia, if you make arrangements ahead of time; certain protocol applies to visits.

International Maple Museum Centre
9753 State Rte. 812, Croghan; (315) 346-1107;
maplemuseumcentre.org; open year-round; admission charged

Anyone interested in NYS history should learn about the maple syrup industry, as NYS is second only to Vermont in maple syrup production in the United States, and Lewis County is one of the top producing counties.

The museum offers the history and evolution of the North American maple syrup industry in the former Leo Memorial Catholic School. Bob and Florence Lamb purchased and donated the old school to the Maple Museum in 1980.

The first floor has a replica of a sugar house, an equipment room, and the American Maple Hall of Fame. A sugar house is also called the boiling shed or sugar shanty, and is where the maple sap is boiled down to syrup in evaporators. There is a room with a wooden storage vat and another room has a variety of sap buckets and bags, birch bark bowls, sap spiles (a tube that goes into the tree and allows the sap to drip into a container), and spouts. The evolution of tubing systems for sap gathering

is also on display. The Maple Hall of Fame room honors those who have achieved the highest recognition in the maple industry.

The second floor has exhibits of early syrup-making techniques and equipment, tin and glass maple syrup containers (they even have one with syrup bottled in 1960), and tons of tin and wood maple candy molds. One room explains why the area where the sugar maple trees stand is named "The Sugar Bush," and another room houses examples of maple syrup evaporators.

The third floor is devoted to displays of logging tools and a replica of a lumber camp kitchen and office. One room is called the Lamb's Room—Lumber Camp and dedicated to Robert and Florence Lamb, who were very generous to the museum. Another room exhibits a lumber camp office and lumberjack bunkhouse. The third room is dedicated to NYS maple queens and ambassadors since 1980. All artifacts are very well marked with descriptive cards.

A couple of unique artifacts include the Sugar Devil, a tool used to break up large blocks of maple sugar that predates the Civil War era, and the Sugar House setup, depicting the scenes of sap collection to syrup production, with many artifacts to represent the process.

"Visitors are often surprised to learn how many gallons of sap, about forty, are needed to process one gallon of maple syrup. Visitors are also frequently interested in the folklore stories of how maple sap was discovered and how a freezing of the sap liquid over periods of freezing weather and removal of ice creates a more highly concentrated maple sap liquid," says the acting board president.

Souvenirs and maple products are available in the gift shop.

Constable Hall
5909 John St., Constableville; (315) 397-2323; constablehall.org; open May through Oct; admission charged

The jewel of the North Country is a two-hundred-year-old Federal-style limestone mansion, built between 1810 and 1819, located on stately grounds in the Adirondack Tug Hill region.

William Constable Sr. "The Purchaser" (1751–1803) bought four million (yes, I triple-checked this figure, four million) acres of land in the Adirondacks at eight cents per acre after he fought for the colonies in the Revolution. He then sold off tracts of land. His son William Constable Jr. "The Builder" (1786–1821) inherited the land and spent nine years building his mansion in the middle of nowhere; sadly he died two years after it was completed. His death was caused by complications due to a wound sustained when a limestone block fell on his leg during the construction of the house. Constable family members resided in the mansion until 1948, and the museum opened in 1949.

Constable Hall houses outstanding artifacts (including a paperweight given to the Constables by Alexander Hamilton) relating to the Constable family and Lewis County. It also maintains gardens and a memorial to persons of Lewis County who fought to preserve our country as a free nation.

Constable Hall is flanked by two outbuildings: the servants' quarters and the carriage house. A beautiful diorama by Frederick N. Keib shows the layout of the Constable estate in 1870.

The gardens are among the oldest in the Northeast, having been continuously gardened since about 1820, and remain in their original form. They are designed in sixteen triangles and walkways that form the shape of St. Andrew's Cross or the flag of St. Patrick. The Constable family valued the connection to both their Irish and Scottish roots. The hedges of Irish blackthorn, which are partially original, were brought to America by William Constable from Ireland as cuttings. A sundial that sits in the midst of the garden was designed and put in place by James Constable in 1876.

According to a trustee: "Constable family tradition says a cousin, Clement Moore, wrote 'A Visit From St. Nicholas,' better known as 'Twas the Night Before Christmas,' for his young cousins growing up at Constable Hall."

A few members of the Constable family are still active in the goings-on of their family's legacy.

Constable Hall offers assorted events throughout the year, such as the annual arts and crafts fair and cruise-in.

Chapman Historical Museum
348 Glen St., Glens Falls; (518) 793-2826; chapmanmuseum.org;
open year-round; admission free, donations appreciated

This Victorian house museum is not your typical museum, as it offers hands-on exhibits pertaining to different aspects of everyday life in the Glens Falls area that are great for the whole family. The standard Victorian decor is still visible through period carpet and wallpapers and some of the furniture.

The home that became the museum was built in the 1860s and later remodeled by hardware merchant Zopher DeLong (1815–1901). Zopher married Catherine Lewis Scott (1819–1891), and they had at least eight children. After Zopher's death one of his sons, John Barker DeLong (1843–1934), took over the home and remodeled it again.

I wondered why the DeLong home was named the Chapman Museum. "The museum was named in honor of Juliet (Goodman) Chapman (1888–1982), who was related by marriage to the DeLong family and the last person to occupy the house. She gave her home to the community to become a local history museum, which was established in 1965 as the Glens Falls Historical Association," says the executive director.

Each room in the museum focuses on a different aspect of life: School Days, Music Memories, Home Style, and Unusual Things, the weird and curious items that make life interesting. Visitor response has been positive to the museum's hands-on exhibits, particularly with younger adults and families with kids, because they get to "do things" and share their own life experiences with one another.

A couple of interesting artifacts are a Victorian human hair wreath, which visitors either find fascinating or disgusting, and an early twentieth-century Victrola, which can be played. Visitors are encouraged to try it out and experience the surprisingly rich sound it produces. Most of the other artifacts are only exhibited for a couple months at a time, so you can visit multiple times and always see something new.

The museum also houses a large collection of Seneca Ray Stoddard images of Lake George, Fort Ticonderoga, Lake Champlain, Glens Falls, and a few select photos of the central Adirondacks.

Seneca Ray Stoddard (1843–1917) is best known for his photographs of the Adirondack Mountains, but he also was a cartographer, writer, poet, artist, traveler, and lecturer. The three thousand–plus photographs in the Chapman Stoddard Collection document not only the Adirondack wilderness but also the human story of the region.

The Chapman Museum Research Archive houses manuscripts, other archival materials, and over ten thousand photographs that document the history of the Glens Falls region.

"What makes the Chapman Museum special is the experience people have with the past. Visitors often comment about the approachable nature of the place. Our goal is for people to be engaged by the things they find, and to have some fun! We want them to touch, try things out, and share their memories with each other. Pictures are encouraged," says the executive director.

Warrensburgh Museum of Local History
3754 Main St., Warrensburg; (518) 623-2928; whs12885.org; open year-round; admission free

This museum focuses on the individuals who pioneered and developed water-powered industries throughout the first century of America's history. Exhibits for preschoolers to adults chronicle Warrensburgh from prehistoric times to the present.

"Visitors are often amazed about the hundreds of jobs in the woods and mills that the early industrialists created, and the numerous Victorian homes, both large and small, those incomes could result in," says the director.

An interesting artifact is a World War I diary handwritten by Joseph Adelbert Aiken. At the time of his enlistment, Joe was a musician and wanted to be in the army band, but wound up being an ambulance driver in Italy and France. The diary (a simple

ruled 8.5 by 11 notebook) is displayed open under glass. Included in this display is an excerpted transcribed version with large type and photos that Joe had taken inserted appropriately. Joseph's 1917–1918 World War I registration card states that he was born April 14, 1889, in West Glens Falls, New York, and his residence was Warrensburg, where he was a pants cutter at the Warrensburg Woolen Company.

In 1894 the United States Post Office ordered that all towns ending in "burgh" drop the "h" some towns complied and some did not. The museum decided to hold on to the "h" of olden days.

Warrensburgh, originally known as The Bridge, became a draw for settlers in the late 1700s because of the area's abundance of forests and the seventy-foot drop in the Schroon River in its last three miles before entering the Hudson River, which made for a great place to harness water. Water power was first used to operate sawmills, in about 1818, for the production of lumber, followed by leather tanning. Wool carding, spinning, and weaving was big because raising sheep was common locally due to the rocky and hilly terrain. High-quality fabrics were produced, as well as work pants and jackets, until about 1950. Paper, pulp, and cardboard manufacturing were important industries until the 1970s. Finished lumber products such as windows, doors, and shutters and even shoe pegs (wooden nails used to sole shoes) were also shipped by the barrel all over the world. Shirt manufacturing, which employed hundreds and was allied with the garment industry of New York City, was the last use of water power, toward the late nineteenth century. The dam was rebuilt in the 1980s and is now a sizable hydroelectric plant pumping into the grid.

Just seeing the 1976 Bicentennial and US flag murals on the sides of the building is worth a visit here.

CAPITAL DISTRICT

New York State Museum
222 Madison Ave., Albany; (518) 474-5877; nysm.nysed.gov;
open year-round; admission free, donation suggested

The New York State Museum offers displays pertaining to all aspects of "The Empire State," covering rural to urban areas. Established in 1836, it is the oldest and largest state museum in the country.

Current permanent exhibits are "Adirondack Wilderness," "American Stoneware from the Weitsman Collection," "Beneath the City: An Archaeological Perspective of Albany," "Bird Hall, Black Capital: Harlem in the 1920s," "Cohoes Mastodon," "Explore New York Map—Interactive," "Fire Engine Hall," "Ice Ages," "M&T Bank New York State Museum Earthquake Center," "New York Metropolis Hall," "Minerals of New York," "Native Peoples of New York," "St. Paul's Chapel: A Place of Refuge," "The World Trade Center: Rescue, Recovery, Response," and "World Trade Center Survivors."

My family and I have visited this museum on and off for about thirty years and we always enjoy it. When my husband and I and our grandsons recently visited, we found aspects of old displays that we had not noticed before and discovered a bunch of new displays. The teenage grandson, who was born in 2002, was enthralled with the 9-11-2001 World Trade Center exhibit, the eleven-year-old's favorite was

the twenty-foot-long Cuvier's beaked whale skeleton and the Cohoes mastodon, and the six-year-old most enjoyed the 1920s recreated classroom from Brooklyn and the burned/crushed fire truck from 9-11. We all liked the real subway car that you can walk through.

A touching component of the World Trade Center exhibit is the Family Trailer that was set up to provide families of the 9-11 victims a private space to view the recovery operations. The trailer is filled with a wide assortment of photos, cards, sympathy posters, and other objects of remembrance.

Interesting artifacts and displays include a 1630 cannon, a replica of an Iroquoian longhouse, a 1929 Franklin automobile built in Syracuse, taxidermy wildlife, an Adirondack lounge chair, a scene and full description of living in a tenement house around 1900, a model of a packet boat (a floating hotel used on the Erie Canal), a replica of a Sesame Street TV set, bicycles from 1870 through 1978, and a paleo-botany collection of Middle Devonian fossils. There is lots of space to roam around in this large museum.

Parking can be an issue in Albany during the week; weekends are easier and cheaper or free.

USS *Slater* Destroyer Escort Historical Museum
Broadway and Quay Streets, Albany; (518) 431-1943; ussslater.org; open Apr through Nov; admission charged for guided tours

This buoyant museum on the Hudson River is the only World War II destroyer escort afloat in the United States. Authentically restored, it offers something for all ages and military buffs.

The USS *Slater* DE766 is a Cannon-class destroyer escort that served in the US Navy during World War II. It is one of 563 similar ships and one of six left in the world that were constructed between 1943 and 1945. Destroyer escorts were a new type of warship built as a result of a critical shortage of antisubmarine vessels in the Atlantic at the outset of World War II. These ships were designed to be maneuverable, high-speed vessels that could be built quickly due to their all-welded construction.

The USS *Slater* helped win the war and served in both the Atlantic and Pacific Theaters during and immediately after the war. Following its World War II service, the ship was deactivated until 1951, when it was transferred to Greece's Hellenic Navy. The *Slater* was renamed *Aetos* and remained in Greek service until 1991, when it was transferred back to the United States under the care of the Destroyer Escort Historical Foundation, which began a painstaking restoration of the ship.

The USS *Slater* arrived at the Intrepid Sea, Air & Space Museum in New York City in 1993, where restoration began, then it was towed to Albany in 1997. The

ship was opened to the public in 1998, still in pretty rough shape, in order to generate operating revenue. The restoration, which still continues, has been an amazing journey, painstakingly fulfilled totally by the volunteers of the Destroyer Escort Historical Museum crew.

"While we have many great artifacts from destroyer escorts, including uniforms, photographs, life rafts, letters home, downed aircraft fragments, and many souvenirs, our favorite artifact is the ship herself. You would be hard-pressed to find a more accurately restored or authentic ship in the historic fleet. We are constantly getting complimented from current Navy officials that our ship could easily pass inspection today," says the visitor engagement and program manager.

The floating museum also offers youth group overnight camping and a historic location to hold naval reunions.

Hart Cluett Museum
57 Second St., Troy; (518) 272-7232; hartcluett.org; open Feb through Dec; admission charged

Visit the "Collar City," as Troy has been called, and learn about the history of the two families that owned this home and Rensselaer County. There are three connected buildings with five galleries, a research library that houses documents dating back to the Revolutionary War, plus fun walking tours and programs.

Amid the nineteenth-century townhouses in the downtown Troy Historic District sits a thirty-room white marble, late Federal-style house constructed in 1827. William Howard built the house as a gift for his only child, Betsey Howard Hart, and her husband, Richard P. Hart. Six decades later the home was sold to the George B. and Amanda C. Cluett family, who resided there for twenty years. In 1910 their nephew, Albert E. Cluett, and his wife Caroline purchased this architectural gem. In 1948 Albert and Caroline bequeathed the Hart-Cluett House to the Hart Cluett Museum (formerly the Rensselaer County Historical Society), and it was deeded to the historical society in 1952.

Cool items that I saw during my visit included a pair of bronze urns made by Tiffany & Company depicting the accomplishments of William H. Frear & Company of Troy, a large 1906 painting/photo of the firemen of the Esek Bussey Station at Tenth and Hoosick Streets by Lloyd Studio, cast-iron stoves, intricate boat models, a Hart Curtain Quarter Coach circa 1830s, the Cluett Sleigh, and the Collar Wagon Body from Berlin, New York, which took collar and cuff piecework to farms outside Berlin in the late nineteenth century.

The "Uncle Sam: The Man in Life and Legend" exhibit is very interesting. Samuel Wilson (1766–1854) and his brother Ebenezer walked to Troy following the American Revolution and at first were brick-makers then went into the meat-packing

business. During the War of 1812, the brothers got a contract to supply the US Army with beef and pork and marked the barrels of meat "U.S." His employees joked that the initials stood for Uncle Sam. "Uncle Sam who? Why Uncle Sam of course! Tis he that's feedin' the whole army!" This is how the legend of one of our national symbols began.

In January 1960 the Veterans for Uncle Sam Committee submitted a petition with over three thousand names to the US Senate, as part of an effort to pass a resolution recognizing Samuel Wilson as the progenitor of Uncle Sam. The resolution, which had already passed in the US House in 1959, was passed in the Senate in 1961. The petition as well as numerous Uncle Sam statues, costumes, and memorabilia are on display.

"Visitors often have no idea that Uncle Sam was based on a real person from Troy. Visitors often comment that they like the whimsy of a past era, evidenced by the 'Ladies Entrance' neon sign from the South End Tavern. Train and history buffs love the extraordinarily well-researched, lifelike Len Tantillo painting of the historic Troy Train Station (in the research library)," says executive director.

An interesting artifact is the Poestenkill Lion painting circa 1840. It was painted on four wide, unfinished boards that had been separated and intended for the fireplace in a house in the town of Poestenkill.

The Hart Cluett Museum also houses the largest local history library, archive, and research center in Rensselaer County. Note that parking is on the street, but we did not have a problem finding a spot.

Knickerbocker Mansion
132 Knickerbocker Rd., Schaghticoke; (518) 664-1700; knickmansion.com; open May through Oct; admission free

It is amazing that this 240-year-old museum, situated in a town that is difficult to pronounce, is still standing. To the best of my knowledge, Schaghticoke is pronounced "Skat-i-coke," and it is the name of a Native American Indian tribe meaning "mingling of the waters," in this case the Hudson and Hoosic Rivers.

This property was occupied by the Knickerbacker/Knickerbocker family, of Dutch origins, for an amazing amount of time, from 1707 until the 1940s. A log home was built by Colonel Johannes Knickerbacker in 1707, then replaced by the brick mansion, now the museum, that was built by Johannes Knickerbacker III (1751–1827) around 1780. Knickerbocker means "master bricklayer," so the material used to build the mansion fits. John Knickerbocker was the last of the family line to own the house when he first rented then sold it to Donald and Rose Weir in about 1940. Local residents gathered in an effort to save the mansion from ruin in about 1957, which lead to the organization of the Knickerbocker Historical Society (KHS) in 1963. KHS eventually purchased the mansion in 1966.

The architecture of the Knickerbocker house was unique for its time, as it was built in the manner of houses in Europe during the Middle Ages. Restoration work on the large portions of the outer walls that had collapsed began in about 1990, and two fireplaces were refurbished in 2012 and 2013. Bringing this diamond in the rough back to its glory days continues to be an ongoing process.

One of the interesting visitors to the house in the early to mid-1800s was the author Washington Irving (his home/museum is also listed in this book), who often visited Herman Knickerbacker. Irving used the pen name Diedrich Knickerbocker for his book *A History of New York* in 1809. After Irving's book became popular, the family spelled their last name with an "o" in the third syllable instead of an "a."

The Witenagemot Oak, or Treaty Tree of Peace and Welfare, located on the Knickerbocker grounds, was planted in 1676 to commemorate the signing of a treaty between New York governor Edmund Andros and the local Mohican people. This is the only "Vale of Peace" on the continent where the Witenagemot, or Assemblage of the Wise (white settlers and Indians), ever assembled for the Native American's welfare. As the core of the massive oak started to deteriorate, people poured cement in the trunk and screwed huge bolts through it in hopes of preserving the tree, but it finally came down during a flood in 1949 at the age of 273 years. What you see on the grounds now is the cement mold of the trunk. My docent told me that according to oral histories, when the tree was in its prime it shaded an acre of land.

A couple of unique aspects of the mansion were pointed out by my docent. Some of the lath used under the plaster on the walls was "accordion lath," which were long boards partly split lengthwise then stretched out. In the front parlor there were three layers of wallpaper; the first layer, which you can see a portion of, was applied in the late 1700s. The ballroom, across the hall, had eleven layers of wallpaper.

The Knickerbocker cemetery is located on the grounds a short distance northwest of the mansion and has graves dating from the early 1700s to the early 1900s.

KHS also provides free genealogical and historical information about the Knickerbocker family and the history of Old Schaghticoke.

New York State Military Museum and Veterans Research Center
61 Lake Ave., Saratoga Springs; (518) 581-5100; dmna.ny.gov; open year-round; admission free

Absolutely everything NYS military, from the Revolution to Desert Storm, can be found at the New York State Military Museum. There's lots of room between the well-organized displays and a Hunting for History scavenger hunt for families, too.

Believe it or not, this museum did not have a permanent home until 2001, even though the collection of artifacts began in 1863 during the Civil War. The collection was often in storage at other arsenals or the NYS capitol building in Albany, and during the 1960s some of it was on display in the capitol. The current museum was the historic Saratoga Springs Armory, designed by Isaac Perry and built between 1889 and 1891. The museum owns the largest collection of state battle flags in the country and the largest collection of Civil War flags in the world, and they still maintain an exhibit of flags at the capitol building.

The museum houses over ten thousand artifacts from the Revolutionary War, Militia Period, War of 1812, Civil War, Spanish-American War, World War I, World War II, Korean War, Cold War, Vietnam War, and Desert Storm. The artifacts include uniforms, weapons, artillery pieces, and art. A significant portion of the museum's collection is from the Civil War. Notable artifacts from this conflict

include the medical kit of Jubal Early's surgeon, and the uniform and bugle of Gustav Schurmann, who was General Philip Kearny's boy bugler. Included in the museum are significant holdings relating to New York's 27th Division in World War I and World War II, and notable state military regiments such as the 7th (Silk Stocking Regiment), 69th (Fighting Irish), 71st, and 369th (Harlem Hell Fighters) New York Infantry.

I visited this museum a few years ago and again recently; both times I was drawn to the Civil War saddle that was used by William H. Leonard of Worcester, Otsego County, New York, a surgeon in the 51st Regiment out of Brooklyn. Two of his brothers, John and George, also served as surgeons in the 51st, and George died of typhoid fever in 1863. Interesting connection: George's uniform and medical kit are housed in the Dr. Christopher Best House in Middleburgh.

I also liked the unique hall stand, the 7th Regiment National Guard New York ballot box from the 1870s, an interesting assortment of helmets, a gas mask circa 1950, medical kits, the fire bucket from the USS *Cumberland*, a draft wheel used for the Civil War draft, and a 1945 Willys MB jeep. My husband found the evolution of guns through the years very interesting.

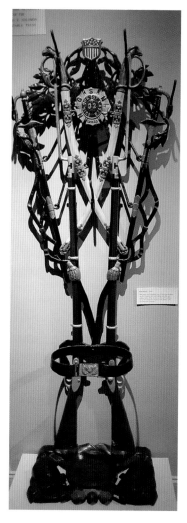

Some interesting objects from the collection are a Civil War frock coat worn by Colonel Elmer Ellsworth and a large mural titled Breaking the Hindenburg Line, painted by George Grey in 1937. Elmer Ellsworth, a Saratoga County native and personal acquaintance of Abraham Lincoln, led his regiment, the 11th New York Volunteers, into Alexandria, Virginia, on May 24, 1861. While in Alexandria during the early morning hours of May 24, Ellsworth climbed to the top of the Marshall House hotel and removed a large Confederate flag. On his descent Ellsworth encountered the hotel's proprietor, who fatally shot Ellsworth in the chest, making him an early martyr for the Union cause. The mural depicts soldiers from New York's own 27th Division during the deadly World War I struggle in September 1918 to break through the German Hindenburg Line, a seemingly impregnable, dense, and complex system of German defenses. Despite the odds and heavy losses, the New Yorkers in the 27th Division fought heroically and successfully broke the line, which significantly weakened the German Army and hastened the end of the war.

An appointment is necessary to visit the Veterans Research Center, which includes a two-thousand-volume library of military and NYS history, over six thousand photographs, unit history files, broadsides, scrapbooks, letters, and maps.

Saratoga National Historical Park
648 Rte. 32, Stillwater; (518) 670-2985; nps.gov; open Memorial Day through Columbus Day for touring the buildings, park is open year-round; admission free

Walk, drive, or bike the grounds of the historic Battles of Saratoga, where you can see the Neilson House or just imagine what it was like to be involved in the "turning point of the American Revolution." "It was here, in 1777, that the British Army surrendered for the first time in world history; it had never happened before, anywhere, anytime," says the park ranger/historian.

Spend as much time as you like at any or all of the ten wayside interpretive stops available on the Battlefield Tour Road. It takes about two hours to drive and stop at

all ten stops and longer, of course, if you choose to bike or walk. Drive time between Saratoga Battlefield and the other sites in the park in the Schuylerville area, where Schuyler House, Saratoga Monument, and Victory Woods are, is approximately fifteen minutes.

Start at the visitor center then proceed to the ten-stop self-guided tour with interpretive signs: Freeman Farm Overlook, Neilson Farm, American River Fortifications (Bemus Heights), Chatfield Farm, Barber Wheatfield, Balcarres Redoubt (Freeman Farm), Breymann Redoubt, Burgoyne's Headquarters, the Great Redoubt, and Fraser Burial Site and Trail. A redoubt is a temporary or supplementary fortification.

The Neilson House was the single-room home of John Neilson that was used as the headquarters for Generals Benedict Arnold and Enoch Poor in 1777. The Schuyler House was the country home of General Philip Schuyler (1733–1804) of the Continental Army, who took part in the Battles of Saratoga. The original house was burned by the British and the house you see now was built in 1777, shortly after British general John Burgoyne's surrender. Schuyler was a farmer and miller. The Schuyler House has many artifacts, most of which are in the form of original eighteenth-century furniture, representative of the types that the Schuylers might have owned.

The Saratoga Monument is a 155-foot stone obelisk that was completed in 1883 and stands where General Burgoyne's camp entrenched during the campaign's final days. If you are able, climb the stairs to the top for a 360-degree view of the Hudson River Valley.

Victory Woods marks the final encampment site for the British Army under General Burgoyne prior to their October 17, 1777, surrender to American forces. The trail is self-guided and offers a raised, accessible half-mile pathway with interpretive signs.

Empire State Aerosciences Museum
250 Rudy Chase Dr., Glenville; (518) 377-2191; esam.org; open year-round; admission charged

A one-of-a-kind museum that has everything to do with just about anything that goes up in the air. When I visited, there were families with children from about age five to teenagers, and all were engaged in some aspect of the museum.

As you drive in you will see in the airpark an F-102 Delta Dagger, F-5E Tiger, F-14 Tomcat, MiG-21 Fishbed, MiG-17 Fresco, MiG-15, F-105G Thunderchief, A-4 Skyhawk, A-10 Thunderbolt II (Warthog), F-4D Phantom, F-101B/F Voodoo, F-84F Thunderstreak, T-2 Buckeye, S-2 Tracker, A-6E Intruder, UH-1 Iroquois (Huey), RA-5C Vigilante, Supermarine Scimitar, F-3D Skynight, A-7E

Corsair, and a 102-foot (half the size of the original) replica of the Concorde, one of the biggest model airplanes in the world. Every aircraft has a descriptive display sign.

The Republic F-105G Thunderchief, my favorite, was one of the most legendary planes of the Vietnam War era and is the largest single-engine ever used by US forces.

Inside the museum you'll find the New York Aviation Hall of Fame, an Amelia Earhart display, World War I aerodrome and aircraft models, Link Trainer, 109th Airlift Wing, Pre-powered flight area, GE Flight Test Center, World War II exhibit, GE Malta Rocket Test Center, NASA lunar rover, and the Jansz Vander Veer Research Center (the research center is open by appointment).

The Amelia Earhart display has a map of her round-the-world route and a mock-up of Amelia's Lockheed 10 that was used in the movie *The Final Flight*. Other displays covered Charles Lindbergh's trans-Atlantic solo flight in 1927, Adirondack bush pilots, the Amundsen-Scott South Pole station, a 1940s aircraft spotter's station, Civil War observation balloons, Pearl Harbor on December 7, 1941, a hot air balloon, the 1902 glider, a Simulated Reality Vehicle (SRV), the X-405 rocket engine, a bomber gun turret, the 18-foot-long model of the Japanese aircraft carrier Akagi, which was used in the movie Tora Tora Tora, and the Curtiss-type Pusher plane flown by nineteen-year-old John Von Pomer of Fort Edward in 1910. The Von Pomer plane was reconstructed with some original parts found in the barn of John's sister Sophia in 1975.

A little side story: My truck driver husband Andy hauled the forty-five-foot-long Concorde nose section from the Cradle of Aviation Museum in Nassau County, New York, to the Empire State Aerosciences Museum in August 2017. The rest of the plane was brought up in sections over the next six months or so.

Even with the tremendous collection of thirty-plus aircraft on display, my teenage grandson liked the one and only army tank the best.

Mabee Farm Historic Site
1100 Main St., Rotterdam Junction; (518) 887-5073; schenectadyhistorical.org; open year-round; admission charged

This is a family-friendly complex of buildings that includes the oldest unaltered house, built in 1705, in the Mohawk Valley.

The property was originally purchased by Daniel Janse VanAntwerpen from the Mohawks in 1671, then Jan Pieterse and Annetje/Anna (Borsboom) Mabee purchased nine acres of the property in 1705. Jan and Annetje had a total of ten children. The eight youngest children were still with them in 1705, and they all lived in the approximately twenty-by-twenty-foot home they built on the property. Mabee family members owned the farm until it was donated to the Schenectady County Historical Society in 1993.

The 1705 stone house was added on to a couple of times, once for additional living space, and later, another building was attached to board travelers for extra household income. Buildings in the complex, besides the original stone house, are the 1790s inn, 1760s brick house, 1760s Dutch barn, small outbuildings for animals, a privy, and the 2011 George E. Franchere Education Center. The original barns burned down, so the hand-pegged H-bent frame Dutch barn you see now was moved from Johnstown (about twenty miles away) in pieces, reassembled, and dedicated in 2001.

During my wintertime visit to the Mabee Farm, the tour guide told me that the brick house basement was a living space for slaves from 1707 to 1827 when NYS abolished slavery. "A crucial fact about the social order of colonial New York is that there was a very familiar, yet strictly hierarchical relationship between free and enslaved," says the educator.

I asked the guide what visitors are most often amazed about, and he told me the size of the Dutch barn and the building style. The guide's favorite artifact is a three-hundred-year-old spinning wheel, housed in the education center, that must have been made by Jan Pieterse Mabee, as it is initialed JPM. My favorite is the eighteenth-century reproduction bateaux (a light, flat-bottomed riverboat), which is housed in the Dutch barn in the winter. There are two bateauxs, named De Sager and Bobbie G., that are available seasonally for boat rides on the Mohawk River, right behind the Mabee house. I was also amazed at the size of the fireplace in the 1705 house, about eight feet wide, and that the hearth was flush with the floor.

While meandering around the Mabee Farm, don't forget to check out the family cemetery, with twenty-one headstones dating from 1771. If visiting in the summer

the farm animals, always fun for the kids, and the orchards and gardens, more for the adults, are enjoyable. Special interactive and lecture programs are also offered throughout the year.

Skene Manor
8 Potters Terrace, Whitehall; (518) 499-1906; skenemanor.org; open Apr through Dec; admission free for guided tours

This elegant Victorian Gothic–style three-story mansion has ten bedrooms, three dining rooms, seven of the eight original fireplaces, and a Tea Room for lunch. The hillside mansion, also referred to as a castle, overlooks the Village of Whitehall and the Champlain Canal.

Judge Joseph H. Potter (1820–1902) had this mansion constructed of gray sandstone, quarried from Skene Mountain, between 1872 and 1874, and called it Mountain Terrace. The Potter family lived in the mansion with their three sons until Joseph's widow Catharine sold it in 1906. The Lowenstein and then Sachs families resided in the grand house until 1939. In 1946 Clayton and Pauline Scheer purchased the castle and converted the downstairs into a restaurant/bar. They renamed the mansion "Skene Manor" in honor of Whitehall's founder, Philip Skene. Mr. and Mrs. J. R. Reynolds continued the restaurant business from 1951 to 1983, then Joel Murphy purchased it and ran the restaurant for a number of years. Skene Manor fell into disrepair after a couple more owners until Skene Manor Preservation Inc. stepped in to restore and maintain it in the mid-1990s.

A guided tour is suggested in order for visitors to enjoy the whole mansion, but guests are able to roam the ground-floor parlor, dining room, library/gift shop, and sitting room on their own. The Potters took their furniture and belongings when they moved, so the mansion is furnished with donated items fitting the late nineteenth-century time period. Furniture in the public rooms of the house is mostly from the 1870s to 1890s. Two of the bedrooms are furnished with East-lake-style beds and dressers, and chairs and sofas in the sitting rooms are generally what is described as Victorian. The sideboard/buffet in the dining room is from 1900 or so. There is an original wallpaper frieze (a horizontal band of sculpted or painted decoration), European in origin, in the entrance hall, dating from the time the house was built in 1874.

"The entire operation, for over twenty years, was conceived by and has been sustained by the Whitehall Skene Manor Preservation Inc. volunteers, who do everything from guiding visitors through the rooms of the house, to preparing and serving

the food that is served in the dining room, to caring for the gardens and grounds. Some visitors are surprised that the Potters would build a nine-thousand-square-foot home in the year that their youngest child graduated from college and moved away, becoming an 'empty nest' home, and a large one, to be sure," says the president of the museum.

Slate Valley Museum
17 Water St., Granville; (518) 642-1417; slatevalleymuseum.org; open year-round; admission charged

Unique would be a good word for this museum, as it celebrates the history and culture of the quarrying community that was established along the New York–Vermont border in the 1800s.

"I really love how the museum explores an industry that is still active today. Many industrial museums explore industries that no longer operate in their communities, but slate is still quarried and milled into an array of different products in our region today. This allows us to explore not only the industry's impact on work, technology, and culture in the past, but through to the present as well," says the interim director.

The museum houses exhibits of historic artifacts, displays revealing the science and art of slate quarrying, a quarry shanty and blacksmith's shop complete with all the machinery and tools used in traditional slate quarrying, a geological display illustrating the natural history of slate, and examples of how slate has been used in the structure and decor of local buildings.

The "Dream and the Reality: Immigration and Assimilation in the Slate Valley of New York and Vermont, 1840 to the Present" exhibit explores the reasons that thousands of immigrants from Wales, Ireland, Slovakia, and Italy came to work in the slate quarries. This area traces what was going on in the old country at the time of immigration, then shifts to the immigrants' new lives in the Slate Valley villages, and includes information on descendants still involved in the slate industry today.

The "Heavy Lifting" exhibit offers a human and technological history of moving slate from quarry to market, 1850 to the present. Some of the artifacts here are a 1951 Mack truck, a 1949 boom and bucket cable-operated shovel, an early 1900s engine and single drum hoist, an early 1900s Owen Jones carriage, and a late 1800s horse-drawn scoop.

The exhibit of Neil Rappaport photographs documents slate company workers from the 1970s through 1990s. In 1993 Rappaport (1942–1998) visited every working quarry and took company portraits for the collection.

A couple of unique items of interest are a mural titled Men Working in Slate Quarry, painted by Martha Levy in 1939, and a slate fan carved by William Pritchard, a Welsh immigrant, in 1896.

"I think that people walk away with an understanding of an industry that they didn't even realize existed. Slate is easy to miss in the world around us, though it has many applications and shows up in many ways, from roofs, to floors, to countertops, to mulch, to home decor. People leave our museum with a greater understanding of the history of the industry, the people who powered it, and the landscape that made it possible. They then begin to notice slate where they did not see it before and how it fits into the world around them," says the interim director.

The museum also offers special programs and events throughout the year.

Delaware County Historical Association & Museum
46549 State Hwy., Delhi; (607) 746-3849; dcha-ny.org; open Memorial Day through Columbus Day; admission charged

One of the buildings in this historic complex is the actual birthplace of Delaware County in 1797. This building is the beautiful old Federal-style Gideon Frisbee House, built in the late 1790s.

Gideon Frisbee (1758–1828) fought in the Revolution, then moved to what became Delaware County in about 1788 and first built a log cabin. He was married twice and had twelve children who all lived, at some point, in the present house. Delaware County Court was convened here for a couple of years until the courthouse was built in the Village of Delhi. Frisbee family members lived in the house until 1960, when the Delaware County Historical Association (DCHA) bought the house and sixty-acre farm.

DCHA was founded in 1945 to preserve and present the rich history of rural America and the folklife of Delaware County through the site's historic buildings, exhibits, and programs. As you walk around the historic Frisbee farm, you can see the original barns, the Frisbee family cemetery (dating back to the 1790s), and

Old Toll Gate, Stamford on the Catskill, N.Y

outbuildings, as well as numerous nineteenth-century buildings from throughout the county that have been moved to the site, including a blacksmith shop, one-room schoolhouse, nineteenth-century gun shop, and turnpike tollgate house, as well as two exhibit galleries, a research library and archive, a gift/book shop, and a nature trail.

The Amos Wood gun shop appears just as it did between 1885 and 1890. The Husted Hollow or Kortright District #10 one-room schoolhouse, built in 1870 and in use until 1933, was moved to the complex from Kortright. The Wooden family blacksmith shop and corn crib was moved from Andes. The tollgate house, which was moved from Stamford in 1968, houses an exhibit titled "A Road Well Traveled: The Susquehanna Turnpike." The exhibit galleries have some permanent—"This Valley Used to Be All Farms"—and rotating exhibits. The Gideon Frisbee House, which was also a tavern and inn at times, has period furnishings including a check-erboard table with corncob checkers and photos of the Frisbee family. If interested in researching Delaware County history or families, stop by the Fletcher Davidson Library (call ahead for times).

"Once tourists have seen the permanent exhibits in the house and in the main gallery, they often express surprise at what they have learned about local history; for example, the frontier aspect of this area in the 1700s, the tensions of the Revolution-ary War, hardiness of the early white settlers, agriculture, transportation, reservoirs, etc.," says the director.

I have been to this complex numerous times, and I have to say they hold the best Civil War reenactment weekend, in June, that I have seen.

Hanford Mills Museum
51 Cty. Hwy., East Meredith; (607) 278-5744; hanfordmills.org; open May through Oct; admission charged

Smell the aroma of fresh-cut lumber as you enter this complex of buildings organized like a mini village of the late 1800s. The space between buildings is short, but enough for children to run off a little steam.

At first there was just a sawmill built by Jonathan Parris in 1846, then there were a couple of owners until Ephraim Douglas bought it in 1858. Ephraim sold it to the Hanfords in 1860, probably because he enlisted in the Civil War. David Josiah Hanford (1834–1899) and his sons, Herbert Willis "Will" (1863–1929) and Horace D. (1870–1959), owned the mill from 1860 to 1945. Hanford Brothers became the name of the mill in 1896 when David's sons took over. The Hanfords added a gristmill, feed mill, woodworking shop, and hardware store. They generated power using waterwheels, water turbines, a steam power plant built in 1881, gas engines, and finally a dynamo that generated electric power. All of East Meredith enjoyed the electricity that the Hanfords first started to generate in 1904. Hanford Brothers Mill turned out lumber, barrel lids, and molding and packing crates, as well as operated a gristmill and feed business. Some of the products made one hundred years ago are still made here today.

Buildings in the complex are the post office building, horse barn, forge/blacksmith, feed mill, boxcar, sawmill and gristmill, hardware store, lumber drying shed, Horace Hanford retirement office, ice house, and John Hanford farmstead. The Cooperstown & Charlotte Valley Railroad trains, which came by the mill starting

in 1900, are gone, but you can still see the railroad bed/rail trail that meanders by Kortright Creek.

Hanford Brothers Mill was purchased by the Pizza brothers, Frank Joe and Mike, in 1945. The mill ceased commercial operations in 1967 and reopened as a museum later in the same year.

"Hanford Mills tells the story of the evolution, operation, and interaction of a mill in a late nineteenth- and early twentieth-century rural community. They can authentically demonstrate about twenty milling processes as they happened historically at the mill. Visitors are often surprised that they can see the entire process of the water wheel and steam power plant using the water from the mill pond to generate the power used to run the woodworking machines, sawmill, and gristmill," says the executive director.

I visited this site years ago and recently attended its Ice Harvest Festival in February with my grandsons. We enjoyed the blacksmith forging a piece of metal into a useful item and the ice carving, and were amazed by the gigantic machinery used to run the mills.

Bronck Museum and Library
90 Cty. Hwy. 42, Coxsackie; (518) 731-6490; gchistory.org; open May through Oct; admission charged

The Bronk Museum complex includes a house said to be the oldest surviving home in Upstate New York, built in 1663 by Pieter and Hilletje Bronck. Can you imagine walking into a house that is over 350 years old?

Pieter Bronck, originally from Sweden, and his wife, Hilletje, originally from Holland, came to the United States in 1652 and settled in Beverwyck, New York, now part of Albany, where they opened a tavern. In 1663 Pieter purchased a tract of land in Coxsackie from the native Mohicans and built his house.

Eight generations of Pieter's descendants passed the ownership of the family dwellings and accompanying farm directly from father to child from 1663 to 1938. Leonard Bronk Lampman, a bachelor, was the last family member to own the property, and upon his death in 1939, he willed the Bronck farm to the Greene County Historical Society. The site has been open to the public as a museum ever since.

"The survival of this site was largely due to its faithful, unbroken ownership of the Bronck family; not even cousins from Cleveland or in-laws ever held title to the Bronck farmstead. The farmstead was sometimes better cared for than at other times, but for the family it was their touchstone. The loyalty of this family to their farmstead for over 275 years is rather remarkable," says the curator.

The Bronck Museum complex consists of the twenty-by-twenty-foot house built in 1663, the stone addition built in 1685, the home built by Pieter's grandson

Leendert Bronck in 1738, a kitchen dependency (detached kitchen), a Northern European side-aisle barn, a Dutch barn, a thirteen-sided hay barn built in the 1830s, and several Victorian-style agricultural buildings.

The converted Victorian horse barn is now home to an exhibit featuring various aspects of Greene County life and the famous model of the Catskill Mountain House, which occupies the entire center of the building.

Since 1963 the Vedder Research Library has served as the archives and special collections of the Greene County Historical Society. The library was named after Jessie Van Vechten Vedder, the first Greene County historian, appointed in 1922.

One interesting artifacts is an ancient split-log table that came from a Greene County Dutch family. "Family tradition indicates that the table dates from the early 1700s and remained in the possession of several generations of the family before entering the museum collection in 1964. The table is primitive and likely made by its original owner. It shows centuries of heavy wear, and is made from a large log that has been split in half, providing a relatively smooth surface. Very few pieces of ordinary early furniture survive, so this table is a bit of a treasure. The wow factor about the Bronck farmstead is that the oldest portion of the Bronck house was 113 years old when the Declaration of Independence was signed," says the curator.

Thomas Cole National Historic Site
218 Spring St., Catskill; (518) 943-7465; thomascole.org; open May through Oct and monthly winter programs; admission charged

This complex of buildings includes the main house where Thomas Cole (1801–1848) lived, the New and the Old Studios where Cole painted, and a visitor center.

"When you step onto the porch at the Thomas Cole National Historic Site and see the sweeping views of the Catskill Mountains that Cole painted, you really understand what this artist was all about. Thomas Cole founded this nation's first major art movement, now known as the Hudson River School. Visitors to the historic site get three experiences in one site: One, it's a historic site, so you get to experience the original spaces where the historic events took place. Two, it's an art museum, and you get to see world-class exhibitions of masterpieces of American landscape painting. Three, it's an experience of nature, as we are surrounded by the stunning natural landscapes that so inspired Cole.

"The Main House is a three-story Federal structure of painted brick that was built in 1815 by brothers Thomas and John Thomson. In 1836, Cole married Maria Bartow, John Thomson's niece, who was living in the house with her uncle and sisters. The newlyweds became part of the household, which included John Thomson, Maria's three unmarried sisters, three of the Coles' children—Theodore, Mary, and Emily—and several hired servants. Cole found spaces to paint in the Main House until 1839 when a studio was created in a storehouse building. He painted some of his most celebrated paintings in this studio, now called the Old Studio, until 1846. The Old Studio is now furnished with his original easels and other art-making equipment," says the executive director.

Cole moved into his New Studio, which he designed, about seventy-five yards from the main house, in 1846. This building was tragically destroyed in 1973 after falling into disrepair. The building you see now is a reconstruction of the original and opened in 2016. The New Studio features a state-of-the-art exhibit space for displaying changing exhibitions and provides a flexible space for lectures and educational programming.

The visitor center is housed in the building that contained the Old Studio. The building, with its original wide floorboards, exposed beams, and bare wood walls, now contains a great variety of books and gifts, and a welcome desk.

"Visitors are often surprised to learn that Thomas Cole was an environmentalist, and that the debate between preservation and development of the land was raging back in his time. This story comes out loud and clear because the Thomas Cole National Historic Site is creating a new model for historic house museums, using digital storytelling hidden within the authentic decor in the historic spaces. Instead of trying to make it look as though the artist has just stepped out, the site is creating immersive visual and audio experiences with the artist's own words and images to make it feel as though Thomas Cole just stepped in," says the executive director.

After Cole's untimely death in 1848, his widow Maria (1813–1884), her three unmarried sisters, and her children Theodore, Mary, Emily, and Thomas Jr. remained at the Cole property, known as Cedar Grove. Theodore lived in the house until his death in 1928. He was the last surviving child of Thomas and Maria Cole.

I stopped by this site while on my way to something else, when it was closed. The buildings are all a few hundred feet apart alongside gravel walkways—very picturesque and cozy.

Museum at Bethel Woods Center for the Arts
200 Hurd Rd., Bethel; (845) 583-2079; bethelwoodscenter.org; open Apr through Dec; admission charged

This is where approximately four hundred thousand people gathered for the Woodstock Festival that took place over fifty years ago August 15–18, 1969. Baby Boomers, who were born in the late 1940s and early 1950s, will enjoy reminiscing here and will want to share those memories with their children and grandchildren.

So why was this long weekend of peace, love, and music called "Woodstock" when it really took place in Bethel? "It was originally supposed to take place in Woodstock and then the organizers also tried for Wallkill, but the local residents turned them down because they were worried about the moral implications of a 'hippie-fest.' Finally Max Yasgur, a dairy farmer, welcomed the youth of America to his alfalfa fields in Bethel," says the assistant curator.

The main exhibit, "Woodstock and the Sixties," offers exhibitions, artifacts, reference materials, and programs for young and old alike. Visitors will learn about the politics, music, art, culture, and societal issues of the 1960s. The Main Exhibit Gallery includes twenty films, five interactive productions, 164 artifacts on display, more than three hundred photographic murals, and dozens of interpretive text panels. Most of your senses will be touched by seeing the iconic fashions of the 1960s, hearing the music from the era, and watching original footage of the historic Woodstock Festival.

In the Corridor Exhibit Gallery, the "3 Days of Peace & Music: The Performers of the Woodstock Festival" exhibit offers vignettes on each of the thirty-two groups that performed at Woodstock. Performers who appeared, from first to last: Richie Havens, Sweetwater, Bert Sommer, Tim Hardin, Ravi Shankar, Melanie, Arlo Guthrie, Joan Baez, Quill, Country Joe McDonald, John B. Sebastian, Keef Hartley Band, Santana, Incredible String Band, Canned Heat, Grateful Dead, Leslie West

& Mountain, Creedence Clearwater Revival, Janis Joplin, Sly & The Family Stone, The Who, Jefferson Airplane, Joe Cocker, Country Joe & The Fish, Ten Years After, Johnny Winter, Blood Sweat and Tears, Crosby Stills Nash & Young, Paul Butterfield Blues Band, Sha Na Na, and Jimi Hendrix.

"When Woodstock alumni come back, they are often very moved when walking on the same spot that they sat, slept, or danced on in 1969. Also, the question that visitors ask the most about the Woodstock Festival is 'How did anyone use the bathroom?' You'll have to visit to find out," says the assistant curator.

As you head out, stop by the Bindy Bazaar Museum Shop and or Yasgur's Farm Cafe, with indoor and seasonal outdoor seating.

Time and the Valleys Museum
332 Main St., Grahamsville; (845) 985-7700; timeandthevalleysmuseum.org; open Memorial Day through Labor Day; admission by donation

This museum complex offers an indoor and outdoor experience with interactive exhibits for all ages that portray the uniqueness of the Rondout and Neversink watersheds.

There's a three-level museum building with exhibits on all floors, plus the 1930s Lost Catskill Farm with a farmhouse, barn, milk house, electric plant, outhouse, spring house, workshop with working waterwheel, a sawmill, granary, ice house, sap house, and chicken coop.

Exhibits include "Tunnels, Toil and Trouble," which covers the history of New York City's complex water system and the towns that were taken to build the system. "Water and the Valleys" covers the history of the Rondout and Neversink Valleys from the prehistory geological periods, Native Americans, early settlers, farming, tanning, and other early industries through the 1930s.

The 1930s Lost Catskill Farm, located behind the museum, tells the story of farmers who were forced to give up their land to build New York City's water system. From the 1930s through the 1950s, over twenty farming communities were lost when NYC came to the Catskills to build reservoirs. Buildings in this recreated farm are furnished with period furniture, equipment, tools, and artifacts. The farm also offers interactive videos, computers, games, and activities for both children and adults. Visitors can even download a mobile app audio tour of the farm that gives the perspective of a ten-year-old's view of the 1930s.

A couple of interesting artifacts are a dog churn that was a labor-saving device used to make butter and a 1930s doll house, with all the original pieces, that was made by two young girls from Eureka, New York. Eureka was one of many hamlets in the Catskills that were removed for the construction of New York City's water supply.

"Visitors are continually amazed at the amount of interesting exhibits available. Visitors are also often shocked when they learn how the area was devastated in order to supply NYC with drinking water. Experiencing the heartache of forced removal of 1,500 Ulster and Sullivan county residents by NYC to build reservoirs, and the complexity of the three branches of NYC's water system, is hard to imagine without being there," says the director.

Hudson River Maritime Museum
50 Rondout Landing, Kingston; (845) 338-0071; hrmm.org; open year-round; admission charged

This museum is dedicated to the preservation and interpretation of the maritime history of the Hudson River, its tributaries, and related industries. Self-guided tours are perfect for families with younger children.

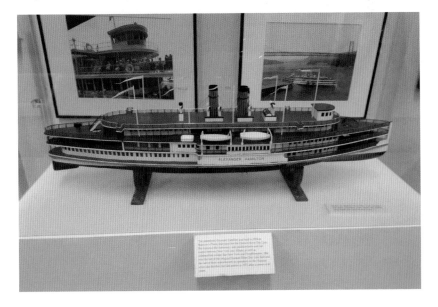

"My favorite aspect of our campus is the location on the Rondout Creek and Hudson River. Not only does it have historical significance of being the site of the famous Cornell Steamboat Co., but we have so many activities available: several exhibit halls, boat-building classes, sailing and rowing classes, and a solar-powered tour boat that takes folks on tours of the creek and river. Most visitors are surprised to hear that we have a lighthouse at the mouth of our creek that was built in the early 1900s and housed lighthouse keepers and their families! These lighthouses kept their tower lights burning to warn vessels away from dangerous navigational points and help vessels find their way in storms. Visitors can take our tour boat for a visit to this remote location and learn about the lives of the light keepers," says the executive director.

According to Cornell's obituary, published in the April 17, 1890, *Port Chester (NY) Journal:* "Thomas Cornell, one of the oldest railroad and steamboat men in the State, died March 30 of pneumonia after a few days illness. He was born in White Plains, Westchester County, January 23, 1814. He was a self-made man, and leaves a large fortune. In 1843 he went to Rondout and a few years later started a steamboat transportation business between that point and New York, which merged into the Cornell Steamboat Company and which is now the largest and most important, company engaged in river transportation in New York State. Mr. Cornell was president of the following named corporations: The Cornell Steamboat Company (1847–1963), the Ulster and Delaware Railroad Company, the Kaaterskill Railroad Company, the Rhinebeck and Kingston Ferry Company, the First National Bank of Rondout, and the Rondout Savings Bank. For years he has also been a director of the Delaware, and

Hudson Canal Company. In politics he was an ardent Republican, and represented the 40th district in Congress (1867–69) and the 47th (1881–83). A widow, Catharine and two daughters survive. Burial in Montrepose Cemetery, Kingston."

Exhibits include historic vessels, objects, archival material, and art related to Hudson River transportation, industries, and recreation such as paintings, prints, photographs, ephemera, blueprints, artifacts, ship models, a one-hundred-year-old shad boat, lifeboats, a lighthouse tender, and ice yachts.

Floor to ceiling, there is something to see at the Maritime Museum. During my family's visit, some of the artifacts we noticed were a display on the sloop Clearwater, America's environmental flagship, including its hand-carved fist tiller; a replica of a canal boat cabin; a gigantic steering wheel; nineteenth-century wooden strap-on ice skates; models of the steamboat Alexander Hamilton and railroad ferry William T. Hart; sailing iceboats; a display of nautical knots, and the last known lifeboat from the steamer Mary Powell, which ran from Kingston to NYS from 1861 to 1917.

Did you know that Kingston was the first NYS capital, for a brief time, in 1777?

Trolley Museum of New York
89 E. Strand St., Kingston; (845) 331-3399; tmny.org; open Apr through Oct; admission charged

Across the street from the Hudson River Maritime Museum is another Kingston treasure—a museum on wheels. View an assortment of trolleys and items that go along with them and then ride a 1920s trolley along the Hudson River.

The Trolley Museum of New York (TMNY) began in Brooklyn in 1955 and survived numerous moves until it landed in Kingston in 1983.

Your museum ticket is good for the museum exhibits, theater, interactive hands-on kids activities, and the trolley ride. The trolley ride departs about every half hour and has three main stops: T. R. Gallo Park, Kingston Point, and the museum itself. There are picnic tables available at every stop where you can enjoy a picnic lunch brought from home, or you can just ride the trolley all day and enjoy the sights. Some of the trolleys on display are from Germany, Belgium, Sweden, and Norway; the oldest was built in 1897.

"Most visitors really enjoy the trolley ride itself, the scenic views of the Hudson River, and the breeze as the car rounds the curve onto the causeway. Our most important artifacts are in the World Trade Center, September 11, collection, which includes a police car crushed by debris, a second completely destroyed, a large amount of debris, and the elevator motor from one of the cars at WTC2. The crown jewel of the collection is the subway car #143, which survived the collapse and is in a relatively intact condition," says the president of the museum.

During our family's visit we first looked around the museum, which has some areas that are a work in progress, and checked out the displays, including one full of conductor's hats and photos. Outside, we climbed the Port Authority Trans Hudson (PATH) Car #143, which was built in 1965 and operated between Manhattan and New Jersey until September 11, 2001. Next we went on the New York City Transit R-16 Car 6398, which was built in 1955 and in service until 1987. Both of these trains are stationary. Since we live in a rural area, my grandsons had never been on trains like this.

The main event of the day was riding on Johnstown Traction Company Trolley No. 358, which was originally an electric trolley built in 1925 and used in Johnstown, Pennsylvania, until 1960. Johnstown was one of the last cities in the United States to abandon street railways. No. 358 next went to Stone Mountain Park in Georgia, where it was used as a tourist ride after it was modified to operate with a diesel engine. The Trolley Museum acquired No. 358 in 1991 and began using it for passengers in 2000 following extensive restorations. During the ride along the Hudson, it was fun to watch all sorts of boats and see the Esopus Lighthouse in the distance. The end of the line is Kingston Point, where the train stops for about ten minutes for passengers to get off and walk around a bit, and for previous passengers to get back on. At Kingston Point there's a little bridge where you can watch the swirling water as Rondout Creek meets the Hudson River. After the little walkabout, back on the train we went for the trip back to the museum.

Phelps Mansion Museum
191 Court St., Binghamton; (607) 722-4873; phelpsmansion.org; open Feb through Dec for guided tours; admission charged

The Phelps Mansion, formerly known as the Monday Afternoon Clubhouse, is a three-story brick and stone mansion built during the Gilded Age in 1870 as the private home of Judge Sherman David Phelps. The Gilded Age was a time of economic boom that took place following the Civil War until about 1900.

Sherman Phelps (1814–1878) married Susan Electa Porter (1823–1843), then married Elizabeth Ann Sweet (1826–1862) and had two sons, Robert and Arthur, and an adopted daughter/niece, Sarah. In October 1873 Sherman and his niece Sara Phelps Ireland sailed to Europe, returning a year later. Sherman's passport described him as five feet nine, dark eyes, Roman nose, and slightly gray hair. At the time of Sherman's death, he was said to be a millionaire who made his money as a businessman and banker. He had also been mayor of Binghamton.

Sherman's children Arthur and Robert, and Robert's wife, Harriett "Hattie" Storey Taylor Phelps, all lived in the mansion until their death (all in their early twenties) between 1880 and 1882. Some believe the spirits of the Phelps family still visit the house. For a number of years Andrew Jackson, a freed slave born about 1848 in North Carolina and coachman for the Phelps family, maintained the mansion after 1882. In 1889 the mansion was sold to George Harry Lester, and in 1905 it was purchased by the Monday Afternoon Club, a women's civic organization. In 1986 ownership of the mansion was transferred to the Phelps Mansion Foundation, but the Monday Afternoon Club continued to meet there until they disbanded in 2006.

The house manager, who was my tour guide, started the tour in the ballroom, which was added on to the original mansion by the Monday Afternoon Club in 1905. The ballroom has a small stage, seating for 125, tiled ceilings, and a very cool chandelier that came from a restaurant in New York City. Most of the furniture and household accessories were donated or purchased to fit the time period. Then we entered one of the parlor rooms, with a unique piano, portraits of the Phelps family, and the first of nine fireplaces, all of which are framed with different types of marble. There is also a portrait of Isaac Gale Perry, the architect of the house. Fireplace mantels, doors, door frames, window casements, stairways, and woodwork are made with an amazing variety of wood: rosewood; fiddleback, birdseye, and quartered maple; mahogany; quartered and burl oak; and walnut and black walnut. There is an abundance of mirrors throughout that make the house look brighter and bigger,

numerous unique chandeliers, carved wood doorknobs, and pocket doors (one set that leads into the sunroom even is partly glass). The dining room has the most interesting wallpaper of metallic peacocks that was installed in 1973, another unique chandelier topped with squirrels, and a never-opened glass case with taxidermy birds shot over 140 years ago by Phelps. Next to the dining room is a commercial kitchen, mixed with older and modern fixtures, which was often utilized by the Monday Afternoon Club and is still used for some special events today.

Upstairs are the bedrooms, a sitting room, and some personal items owned by Sherman and his granddaughter Lucretia Phelps. In the second-floor hallway are a bunch of canceled checks in a frame. The checks were cashed by speakers that spoke at Monday Afternoon Club meetings. One of the checks was endorsed by Amelia Earhart in 1935, two years before she disappeared. She was paid $250, big bucks for 1935.

The third floor originally included a billiards room, servants (there were usually five) quarters, and storage. "Nine out of ten visitors are surprised that the third floor was removed in 1941, due to a water leak, and replaced with a replicated facade in 2002 that cost $750,000," says the house manager. I too was amazed when I saw a picture of the two versions of the mansion.

Roberson Museum and Science Center
30 Front St., Binghamton; (888) 269-5325; roberson.org;
open year-round; admission charged

History and science, old and new, are combined at the old Roberson estate. All ages will find something of interest here.

The Italian Renaissance Revival–style house that became the museum was built and completed in 1907 for Alonzo Roberson Jr. (1861–1934). "Since the house was built in the early twentieth century when electric lighting was relatively new, Roberson was somewhat doubtful about the new technology but did not want to be on the wrong side of the fad. Consequently, he had his home equipped with both electric light and gaslight. Many of the original custom light fixtures remain, and you can see how they were plumbed for gas and wired for electric. The coffered (a coffer in architecture is a series of sunken panels) ceiling in the dining room features what looks like murals painted on plaster, but it's actually painted, stretched canvas between the beams. Similarly, the foyer ceiling is covered in suede and the wall covering in the living room is also a stretched fabric. While Mr. Roberson made his fortune in lumber and casework, the use of textiles as part of the interior design indicates that he was very concerned about comfort; these few details would help reduce sound transfer and also provide an amount of insulation. The house does hold a temperature remarkably well all year," says the executive director.

The mansion opened to the public in 1954 as a museum called the Roberson Memorial Center; the Martin Wing, with the region's only digital planetarium was added in the late 1960s; the A. Ward Ford Wing, which houses the Decker Life Science Center, was added in 1984; and most recently the Roberson's carriage house, which houses a pottery studio, was renovated in 1996.

"The Roberson Mansion was gifted to the community in the will of Alonzo Roberson Jr., once his wife Margaret (1866–1953) was done using the house. It was Roberson's wish that the house become a community hub of learning. For more than a decade it was just that: Servants' quarters were converted to offices; classes in dance, painting, and photography were offered; and the Board of Trustees met around the dining room table. It was community-driven and collegial. The massive modern addition that was built in the 1960s was added to accommodate gallery space, a large performance space, and proper offices. The house wasn't intended to be a historic home that was stuck in time, it was meant to be well used and well loved. In its century standing on Front Street, it has certainly fulfilled the original owners' desires," says the executive director.

The mansion features a restored third-floor ballroom, a stunning grand staircase, twenty-six rooms, eleven fireplaces, and a working wrought-iron elevator.

Exhibit areas include "Haudenosaunee: People of the Longhouse," where visitors can explore the history and culture of these Native American people—their beliefs and philosophy, relationship with the land, and association with the Europeans who migrated to North America; "NatureTrek," an exploration and celebration of the natural world that surrounds us, anchored by over 150 mounted specimens from the Robersons' Lee J. Loomis collection; "The Legacy of Edwin A. Link," which includes examples of his amazing advancements as a pioneer in aviation, underwater archaeology, and submersibles; and "Expanded Model Train Layout," the region's largest public model train display depicting the 1950s era.

Chenango County Historical Society Museum and Campus
45 Rexford St., Norwich; (607) 334-9227; chenangohistorical.org; open Feb through Dec; admission free, donations appreciated

Visitors will be amazed by the stained-glass doors that greet you before entering this spacious museum. There is plenty of room for families to meander from one exhibit area to the next.

The exhibits at this museum explore the local culture of Chenango County and the central New York region from prehistory through the present, with a special emphasis on Native American history, industrial history, settlement and migration, transportation, and agriculture.

The museum is housed in the former Ward School #2, which was built in 1896 and used to teach scholars until 1957. In 1958 the Chenango County Historical Society, which was established in 1939, bought the old school, gathered and moved its artifacts, and opened the museum in 1962.

The other structures that are part of the Chenango County Historical Society campus are the Ross one-room schoolhouse and privy from Preston and the Loomis Barn from Tyner; a maple sugar house; the Chenango Canal building, home to packet boat model "The "Lillie"; and the Flanagan Research Center.

During my visit to the museum I found some totally unique items and galleries. The Commerce Gallery featured exhibits pertaining to NBT Bank, N.A. (founded in 1856 and originally called the Bank of Norwich) and the Norwich Pharmacal Company. Among the many interesting artifacts, my favorites were a pill-coating pan (for coating pills) used in the 1930s to 1940s, displays of pharmaceutical products, and a bank teller's window.

In the 1865–1917 Gallery I found a kitchen area complete with a cast-iron stove, a beautiful dining room area, Victorian human hair wreaths, and a hand-carved pipe holder with tobacco box circa 1890 referred to as Tramp Art. In between this gallery and the next was the Native American/Indigenous Heritage Gallery, displaying clothing and assorted artifacts.

In the Upper East Gallery the items that caught my eye were the tin bathtub with back rest, the specially made ash holder (ashes were used for polishing silver), the Methodist Church library bookcase, looms, old rifles, and an oxcart from the early 1800s.

The "Fifty Stories" room displays fifty people, places, or things, with fifty-word description cards, pertaining to Chenango County. The items that I found most unique were a Chenango County Highway Department time clock circa 1910, a 114th Regiment hand-stitched American flag, and a Mickey Mouse pot holder circa 1932 made by the Norwich Knitting Company. Norwich's collaboration with Walt Disney Enterprises to make Mickey Mouse and other Disney character textile goods helped Norwich rise out of the Great Depression. This is one of the executive director's favorites. About 150 more scenarios are all prepared and ready to be rotated through this exhibit to keep it new and interesting for repeat visitors.

The museum also features a gift shop filled with one-of-a-kind gifts, as well as publications on local and regional history that cannot be found elsewhere. Across from the gift shop is a revolving gallery with the most incredible and unique display cases.

Northeast Classic Car Museum
24 Rexford St., Norwich; (607) 334-2886; classiccarmuseum.org; open year-round; admission charged

As you can tell by the name of this museum, they have cars, but not just a handful of cars, they have two hundred-plus cars, trucks, motorcycles, and airplane engines, plus vintage clothing, gas pumps, and even a camper.

When I walked into this eighty-nine-thousand-square-foot museum with five connecting buildings on one floor and saw all the glistening shiny cars my first thought was imagining who has to dust all of these cars. Almost one hundred volunteers keep this museum in top shape.

Each of the exhibit rooms has a different group of cars: "Those '70s Cars" has antique cars from the 1970s; "Post-War Collection" has vehicles from the late 1940s through early 1960s, including Desoto, Studebaker, Windsor, Nash, Crosley, and Hudson; "Tribute to Bennett-Ireland" is dedicated to all the companies that operated out of the building, including the Norwich Wire Works, Ireland Machine and Foundry Company, Bennett Fireplace Company, and Bennett-Ireland; and "Made in New York" has examples of cars made all over NYS, such as the Playboy, Mora, O-we-go, Pierce Arrow, and Chenango Camper.

The "Fabulous Franklins" exhibit features the largest collection of Franklins anywhere, including the third one built and the last. The Franklins are part of the George E. Staley Collection. Staley was instrumental in the formation and opening of the museum in 1997. Franklins were made between 1902 and 1934 in Syracuse, New York. The Franklin Automobile Company began when Herbert Henry Franklin (1866–1956), a bachelor, teamed up with John Wilkinson, who had invented an

air-cooled motor. He turned out twelve cars in 1902 and nearly fifteen thousand in 1929, then went bankrupt in 1934 in part due to the Depression.

The "Pre-War Collection" includes electric, steam and combustible engine vehicles such as Knox, Model T, Scripps Booth, Hupmobile, Duesenberg, Packard, and a 1930 Henderson motorcycle. The operations assistant told me that the museum is continually changing vehicles in the "Pre-War," "Post-War" and the "Made in New York" exhibits so there is always something new to see.

"Vintage Airplane Engines" from World War I and World War II includes the eighteen-cylinder R-3350 Turbo B-29 Super Fortress Bomber engine.

It is truly amazing how they fit so many cars into one facility and still have spacious aisles to walk around them all (they offer scooters, on a first-come, first-served basis, at no additional cost, too). Understandably, visitors can not touch any of the cars, but there is one, a 1933 Franklin Olympic, that you can sit in and use for a photo op. This car has a small fan on the steering column for air conditioning and the face of a wrist watch implanted in the rear view mirror.

My favorite car was a 1975 Chevrolet Cosworth Vega, my husband's favorite was a 1932 V-16 Cadillac (can you imagine keeping sixteen cylinders timed), and the two tour guides' favorites were a 1950 Desoto and 1957 Buick convertible.

There is an interesting collaboration between the Northeast Classic Car Museum and the Chenango Historical Society Museum in that the manikins spread around the car museum are dressed in period clothing provided by the Chenango Historical Society.

Visitors often describe the museum as a "hidden gem," according to the operations assistant, because they had no idea there was such a wide variety of rare and unique vehicles tucked away in rural NYS.

Madison County Historical Society, Cottage Lawn Museum
435 Main St., Oneida; (315) 363-4136; mchs1900.org; open year-round; admission charged

The society's headquarters, Cottage Lawn, is an 1849 Gothic Revival villa designed by prominent architect Alexander Jackson Davis for Niles Higinbotham.

Niles Higinbotham (1812–1890) came to the village of Oneida about 1844. His father Sands is considered to be the founder of the Village of Oneida. Niles married Eliza Randall (1823–1903) on October 30, 1849, and they had three daughters Julia, Louise, and Eliza/Lilly, who all became spinsters. Niles was one of the contractors in building the Erie railroad, and was a co-founder of the Oneida Valley National Bank in 1851 and president of the bank for thirty-nine years, until his death. Eliza and her daughters Lily and Louise were among the sixty-four charter members that established the Madison County Historical Society in 1898. The last surviving daughter, Louise, who lived in the house, willed the home to the Madison County Historical Society in 1931.

The 5,706-square-foot Cottage Lawn museum, which took 103,590 bricks to build, is furnished with Victorian period pieces from the Higinbotham collection and artifacts from Madison County's fifteen towns and city. The museum has two parlors, a dining room, library/trophy room, kitchen with butler's pantry, vault,

children's room, grandmother's room, servant's room, and a room with changing exhibits. Sadly, the Higinbotham household contents were auctioned off in 1931, but many items have made their way back. On the grounds in the agricultural barn is an exhibit on hop culture in Madison County.

On my guided tour through Cottage Lawn, I saw interesting artifacts such as musical instruments including three pianos, one of which was a miniature for a wheelchair-bound daughter to use in bed; numerous Victorian taxidermy dioramas, donated mostly from the Maxon family, in glass cases and domes, including one with a blowfish; unique stained-glass doors; shutters on the inside because Niles Higinbotham thought they were a detriment to the beauty of the exterior; a Timby Solar clock circa 1865; a papier-mâché end table; fine China with a hop pattern; a mammy/nanny bench rocker; Victorian hair wreaths; the bank vault of the first bank in Oneida; a dual wood and gas cookstove; a Napoleon Cigar (made in Oneida by Powell & Goldstein, 1879–1943) display; and Native American beadwork "Whimsies." When departing from the house, check out the amazing variety of huge trees in the front lawn.

The society also operates the Mary King Genealogical Research Library.

Walter Elwood Museum of the Mohawk Valley and ALCO Historical & Technical Society
100 Church St., Amsterdam; (518) 843-5151; ahts.org and walterelwoodmuseum.org; open year-round; admission free

Roam at your own pace in this marvelous eclectic mix of artifacts. Even the building itself is eclectic, with walls of local limestone dating back to 1842, plaster, brick, or cement, and stained-glass windows and beautiful doorways thrown in here and there.

The Walter Elwood Museum began as the Children's Museum that Walter created in the Amsterdam Fifth Ward School in 1939. Walter Elwood (1886–1955) was a teacher in the Philippine Islands from 1908 to 1911, was a Red Cross volunteer in France during World War I, and was associated with Amsterdam schools from 1935 to 1955. The artifacts in the museum were mostly collected during Walter's travels around the world. He continued traveling and collecting along with his wife, Anne Bevillard (Mack) Elwood, after their marriage in 1926.

The museum, housed in the former Noteworthy Complex, Sanford & Sons Carpet Mills, which prior to 1842 was a lumber mill building, holds approximately twenty-five thousand artifacts that fall into four main categories: multicultural, Victorian, natural history, and items that relate to the Mohawk Valley.

There is a picture room with portraits or photos of numerous noteworthy citizens of the area. The Vintage Children's room has toys and games spanning a couple of hundred years. A Complicated Weave room features the history of carpet manufacturing in Amsterdam. There is a Military room with uniforms and implements from all the wars. The Natural History Animal room houses an abundance of taxidermied animals, from birds to mammals, including an anteater and an elephant's foot. The Research room is loaded with a wide assortment of old books. The Community room has spinning wheels, phonographs, doll houses, baby/doll carriages, typewriters, a display on the Temple of Israel, and bicycles. The Native American conference room houses a plethora of beautifully displayed artifacts.

I asked the office assistant, who showed me around, what her favorite item was, and she said, "The Noteworthy Kaleidoscope." When I first saw it I had no idea what in the world it was supposed to be. Employees and subcontractors of Noteworthy Industries of Amsterdam made it in 1996. It is a unique kaleidoscope that stands about six feet tall—and it works. The wheels are a one-of-a-kind stained-glass design, and the stand is made of cherrywood and multiple metals then brass plated. The kaleidoscope is said to be the second largest in the world.

"Some of the unique aspects of our museum are a collection of paintings by Mary Vander Veer, a world-renowned artist; one-of-a-kind custom Tiffany lamp with hand-painted glass slides made for Robert Frothingham, world traveler/collector and hunter; polar bear and brown bear rugs with head and claws; and a walrus with thirty-two-inch-long tusks. The bears and walrus came from the Robert Frothingham collections and were hunted personally by him," says the executive director.

Most of the rooms are sprinkled with artifacts showcasing the Lithuanian heritage in Amsterdam, said to be the most Lithuanian city in NYS.

The "ALCO Heritage" exhibit features everything to do with trains. My favorite artifact was a model of an ALCO 5200, the Mighty Hudson, built by Charles W. Lester, who was an ALCO draftsman and model train builder.

The American Locomotive Company (ALCO), based in Schenectady, was formed in 1901 with the merger of Schenectady Locomotive Works and seven smaller locomotive manufacturers. ALCO was the second-largest steam locomotive builder in the United States, and they went on to build diesel-electric locomotives until 1955 when the company was sold; it closed in 1969.

Be sure you look all around as you stroll through this interesting museum, as there are hidden treasures everywhere.

Fort Klock Historic Restoration
7203 Rte. 5, St. Johnsville; (518) 568-7779; fortklockrestoration.org; open May through Columbus Day; admission charged

Fort Klock is surrounded by a complex of assorted outbuildings nestled in the Mohawk Valley. The main tour, which is enjoyable for all ages, takes place in the 260-year-old Klock-fortified homestead that was built of limestone in 1750 by Johannes Klock, a German Palatine.

Generations of Klock family members lived on the property until 1936 when Lipe Klock died. The property remained in the family but was abandoned and fell into disrepair until the newly formed Tryon County Muzzleloaders worked out a deal in 1953 to use the house as a meeting place if they restored it. Tours began in 1961.

As I drove into the Klock property I noticed the restored schoolhouse circa 1825; the Dutch barn circa 1790, which was moved to the complex in 1989 and reassembled; and the blacksmith shop and mid-nineteenth-century "cheese house," which are utilized for special occasions. At the bottom of the hill is the homestead that also doubled as a fort during the French and Indian War (1754–1763) and the American Revolution (1775–1783).

The tour guide greeted me at what I thought was the front of the house but turned out to be the back. The front faces the Mohawk River where neighbors or those searching for refuge in the fort would have docked. My tour started in the kitchen, which was a 1760s addition to the house, where there is a wide assortment of implements, dishes, and a hand-carved stone sink that had been discarded out on the property. While looking around the kitchen, I noticed some eight-by-ten-inch holes in the wall with hunks of wood in them about four feet up from the floor. They turned out to be musket loopholes, used to stick a musket through and fend off attackers. The next room we visited was a living/meeting space that houses an assortment of artifacts, a dining room table, and a small weaving loom. The last room on the first floor was the original kitchen and is now the gift shop with a full-size canoe hanging from the ceiling, animal pelts hanging on the wall, and a display titled "Mohawk Valley, Breadbasket of the Revolution."

On the second floor there is a room set up as a bedroom including a foot and bed warmer and a commode that held a chamber pot. The tour guide said most of the contents of the chamber pot would be thrown outside, but some of the urine was saved to make saltpeter, an ingredient for making gunpowder. The next room is filled with tools and implements such as brooms made strictly with a birch log, wood shovels, adzes (a sideways axe for trimming beams), a dog treadmill, pails, a cabbage slicer, and my and the tour guide's favorite, a shingle trimmer. The third and final room housed everything to do with weaving: loom, swift, bobbin winder, spools and skarne (for holding multiple spools), mill, and shuttle. My favorite was seeing flax in its natural form being transformed into thread for making linen. As we were leaving the second floor, the tour guide pointed up to the attic where the militia men often stayed.

On my way out I took a walk around the premises and noticed the interesting beehive oven, the little stream running through the property, and the Mohawk River off in the distance.

Oneida Community Mansion House
170 Kenwood Ave., Oneida; (315) 363-0745;
oneidacommunity.org; open year-round, guided and unguided tours
in the summer; admission charged

It is hard to believe that there was a commune in the middle of NYS in the mid-1800s, but that is exactly what the Oneida Community Mansion was built for. All who lived in this community shared the property, the work, the mansion, love, equal status, partners, and the responsibility of raising the children.

John Humphrey Noyes founded and led his Oneida followers, from 1848 to 1880, with a doctrine that was free of sin titled Perfectionism. Newspaper articles used other names for Noyes's religious-based group, such as communists, bible communists, free love colony, commune, experiment in human stirpiculture, experiment in community living, socialist utopia, and radical cult social system. Stirpiculture was a term Noyes used to refer to his system of eugenics, or the breeding of humans to achieve desired perfections within the species.

John Humphrey Noyes was born in 1811 into a family of means in Brattleboro, Vermont. He graduated from Dartmouth College then went to Andover and Yale Theological Seminaries and earned a license to preach in about 1833, but it was revoked soon afterward due to his radical revivalist views. Noyes continued preaching his philosophy around the New England area and started a Perfectionist colony in Putney, Vermont, in the 1840s. In October 1847 he was arrested for adultery, and while awaiting trial Noyes and about forty followers traveled to Oneida.

The ninety-three-thousand-square-foot Mansion House was built in stages between 1861 and 1878. Census reports list the "Oneida Community" population as totaling 163 members in 1855, 210 in 1860, and 237 in 1875. John's wife Harriet, whom he married in 1838 in Vermont, was listed with fourteen children, mostly born by other women, in the 1875 census. The community found farming to be unprofitable so moved on to manufacturing animal traps (they sold over two hundred thousand traps per year in the early 1860s), chains, silk thread, canned fruits and vegetables, and printed booklets. Their most successful endeavor was silverware, which became their main product in 1910.

The Oneida Community folded in 1880 due to internal and external conflicts. John handed over the reins to his son Theodore in 1876, but it did not go well. In 1879 John fled to Canada after hearing that the authorities were planning on arresting him and the surrounding communities were starting an uprising against him and his followers. The former Oneida Community members formed a joint-stock corporation, Oneida Community Ltd. in 1880, which became Oneida Ltd. in 1935 and achieved world-wide recognition for the tableware it produced in Sherrill, New York. Ex-members continued to live in the mansion and also rented rooms out. The mansion has been continually inhabited since 1862.

Oneida Community Mansion House collections include family portraits, historical photographs, period furniture, braided tapestries, books, Community-designed clothing, and ephemera that illustrate the intellectual, cultural, and business life of the Oneida Community. There are permanent and changing exhibits and period rooms such as the Sleeping room, Sitting room, the Community's library, Community Hall, and the nursery kitchen. The Hall has a stage, balcony seating, and paintings of Greek Muses on the ceiling.

"The Big Hall was the setting for daily evening meetings of the Community where spiritual and practical guidance was shared. The same room hosted ambitious performances in the nineteenth century for the three-hundred-member Community and the public. They performed George Bernard Shaw, featured their own orchestra, and reveled in culture and the arts. Today, the space hosts performances including the Mansion House Music Series and theatrical performances," says the executive director.

Some of the interesting items I noticed during my visit were a diorama of the whole mansion, a huge (5 feet 1½ inches by 6 feet 9¼ inches) puzzle of West Point made with approximately ten thousand pieces in 1928, a carpet bag made by the Community in the 1860s, Oneida Plate and Stainless spoon displays, a cabinet of curiosities, and a hands-on display of Kinsley's braiding technique.

The "Braidings of Jessie Catherine Kinsley" exhibit features her exquisite, one-of-a-kind braided silk tapestries that she created from 1908 to 1938. Jessie Catherine (Baker) Kinsley (1858–1938) was born in the Community, married another Community member, Myron Kinsley, in 1880, then lived in a few different places before returning to Oneida. You will also find Kinsley artwork hung here and there as you meander around the museum.

Another exhibit, the "Oneida Game Traps, 1852–1925: The Edward J. Knobloch Collection," displays more than fifty types of traps and illustrates how local trap-making began with the Oneida Community. These traps are made of steel and used to catch animals remotely for food or pelts.

Visitors are also welcome to stroll around the beautifully landscaped thirty-three acres of lawns and gardens, and can even book an overnight stay if interested. There are also some occupied apartments in the mansion, so watch for signs noting private quarters.

H. P. Sears Oil Co. Inc. Service Station Museum
201 N. George St., Rome; (315) 335-5633; hpsearsoil.com; open May through Sept; admission free

Visit a one-of-a-kind completely restored service station built by Howard P. Sears Sr. in 1929.

Howard P. Sears (1896–1984) moved from Bombay, New York, to Rome with his parents, Thomas and Jennie, and brothers Floyd and Kyle Sears in 1900. At the age of fourteen, Howard started a bicycle sales business and the next year started selling automobile accessories. By 1919 he was selling gasoline. He married Marion A. Sexton (1906–2001) in 1922, and they had at least four children. Howard built his first service station in Utica (1928–1929), then built the station that became the museum. At least seven more stations followed until 1939.

"By far a favorite aspect of the site is the patience and perseverance of brothers Howard Jr. and Tom Sears. They decided when they closed the original station in 1974 that one day they would turn it into a museum in honor of their father, Howard P. Sears Sr., who founded the Sears Oil Company in Rome a century ago. Their dream was realized in 2005 with the opening of the H. P. Sears Oil Co. Museum.

"With its unusual terracotta tile roof and white stucco exterior decorated with bright blue and red porcelain steel tiles, the building in downtown Rome is a head-turning architectural and historical jewel. It was recognized by the regional Landmark Society shortly after it opened to the public," says the volunteer manager.

The wow factor for many visitors comes when they learn that the Sears Oil Co. is not and never has been associated with the famous Sears Roebuck and Co. It is named for the Sears family of Rome, and it has withstood more than one lawsuit by the "other" Sears attempting to get the local company's name changed.

The station still has the original oil change pit, restored clock-face gas pumps topped with illuminated glass globes, four pumps offering various grades of gas and kerosene, and Toledo air scales. Inside are an assortment of oil cans and spouts, attendants' hats, photos, and newspaper clippings.

Howard P. Sears's motto was "A Superior Product at Less than Ordinary Gas Prices."

Oneida County History Center
1608 Genesee St., Utica; (315) 735-3642; oneidacountyhistory.org; open year-round; admission free, donations encouraged

This museum has been offering the heritage of Oneida County and the upper Mohawk River Valley since 1876. A roomy five-thousand-square-foot gallery has multiple exhibits running concurrently.

"Oneida County has a deep, rich history with many national connections. The first section of the Erie Canal, which was completed in Oneida County in 1819, went from Rome to Utica, and the Saturday Globe of Utica is home to the first newspaper with color illustrations. Many famous residents once called Oneida County home including Vice President James Schoolcraft Sherman, founder of Kodak George Eastman, major general and composer of 'Taps' Daniel Butterfield, Senator Roscoe Conkling, and Governor Horatio Seymour," says the director of education and outreach.

Interesting artifacts include the Mohawk Lamp, a kerosene lantern that was used to mark navigable channels and enabled canal boats to travel safely along the Erie Canal and other NYS canals. This lantern still contained kerosene when it was donated to the Oneida County Historical Society in 2007. The lamp was manufactured by Dressel of Arlington, New Jersey, in the late nineteenth or early twentieth century. Another artifact is an Erie Canal packet boat ticket, dated July 3, 1848, which was good for one trip from Utica to Syracuse on the Erie Canal. The ticket cost just $1.50. Finally, the Staffordshire Pitcher is a ceramic vessel that was created in 1824 to commemorate the "soon-to-be-opened" Erie Canal, which officially opened, from Albany to Buffalo, in 1825. The reverse side of this pitcher pays homage to the fast-growing city of Utica, which expanded substantially after the canal's construction.

These three artifacts were chosen for their historical significance—both local and state. The Erie Canal, and later the Barge Canal, shaped the development of Oneida County, the Mohawk Valley, and New York State. This revolutionary development sparked economic prosperity in the region and enabled relatively "quick" transportation from New York City to the Great Lakes and beyond.

The Akkadian Cuneiform block is one of the oldest items in the history center's collection. It likely traveled from ancient Mesopotamia to the United States and ended up in Utica by way of Ninevah. It holds an ancient message in a form of writing called cuneiform, which is produced using a pointed rod to leave indentations in clay. The identification tag originally listed the block as Egyptian hieroglyphics; however, the writing was recently identified as cuneiform of Akkadian dialect, and translation revealed its age to be around almost three thousand years old! The text praises King Shalmanezer V (726–722 BC), who is mentioned in the book of 2nd Kings in the Bible. The block is believed to be a practice block due to the quality of the indentations.

If interested in historical or genealogical research during your visit, the Colonel Tharratt Gilbert Best Research Library contains over 250,000 documents and books, and tens of thousands of images.

Hyde Hall
267 Glimmerglass State Park, Springfield; (607) 547-5098; hydehall.org; open Memorial Day through Oct for guided tours; admission charged

If you are interested in bygone architecture, visit this incredible neoclassical country mansion of nearly fifty rooms, built between 1817 and 1834, tucked away above Glimmerglass State Park with a beautiful view of Otsego Lake. Bring a swimsuit when you visit here, as you can jump in the lake, with a sandy beach, after your tour.

I had been to Glimmerglass State Park for swimming and picnic lunches through the years, but had no idea about Hyde Hall until I looked up the hill and there it was.

The mansion was built for George Clarke (1768–1835), who had left England and moved to Albany in 1806, then purchased 340 acres for the construction of his country villa, Hyde Hall. The next generations to take over Hyde Hall were George Jr. (1822–1889), George Hyde Clarke (1858–1914), George Hyde Clarke Jr. (1889–1955), and finally, Thomas Hyde Clarke (1936–2015). It is said that Ann Low (Cary) Clarke (1780–1850), wife of the George who built Hyde Hall, haunts the mansion. In 1963 the mansion and six hundred surrounding acres passed to NYS as a result of eminent domain proceedings to create Glimmerglass State Park. The Friends of Hyde Hall was formed in 1964 to save the house.

Following are some interesting aspects of the mansion: The balcony railing was made by master blacksmith Amos Fish of Albany, in 1833. The courtyard has a projecting, semicircular bay that contains the main staircase to the second and third floors of the Great House. The courtyard allowed light and air to the interior rooms, separating the family areas from the guest and staff areas, and holds a cistern that was supplied with water from the roofs. The main staircase is a gorgeous circular staircase. The portico of the Great House is one of the earliest uses of the Greek

Doric order in NYS. A portico is a structure consisting of a roof supported by columns at regular intervals, typically attached as a porch to a building.

Numerous furnishings in the mansion are originals, documented by Clarke's meticulous recordkeeping, such as his 1813 dining room table and sideboard. Each generation of Clarkes also left furnishings that reflected their time spent at Hyde Hall.

Hyde Hall's 1820s Tin Top Gatehouse, which originally gave entrance to the extensive landscaped grounds of the estate and led up to the front of the mansion, returned to that function in 2015 as a visitor center that houses the ticket office, bookstore, and exhibit space.

Another interesting building on the Hyde Hall estate is a fifty-three-foot-long, Burr Arch Truss–style covered bridge, built in 1825, that crosses Shadow Brook and is said to be the oldest covered bridge in NYS.

"Hyde Hall has an extensive collection of original furnishings by John Meads, an Albany, New York, cabinetmaker. These furnishings, which were commissioned by George Clark in the 1820s and 1830s, include case pieces, sideboards, tables, chairs, and bedsteads. Hyde Hall is home to the largest collection of Meads furnishing in the United States. There are also numerous pieces by New York City cabinetmakers Duncan Phyfe and Joseph Meeks. Current restoration efforts are concentrating on the era of George Clarke (1768–1835). Wilton carpets, upholstery, and drapery fabrics have been carefully reproduced in order to present the house as it would have looked in his lifetime. Hyde Hall's drawing room and dining room were the largest in a private home west of Albany, New York, when completed," says a past long-term board member.

Swart–Wilcox House Museum

Wilcox Ave. (next to Riverside School), Oneonta; (607) 287-7011; swartwilcoxhouse.wordpress.com; open July and Aug or by appointment; admission free, donations accepted

This German Palatine vernacular house, now a museum, is the oldest house in the city of Oneonta, built in 1807 on the banks of the Susquehanna River by a Revolutionary War soldier. A vernacular house was built in the style of the Palatine region of Germany, in the tradition of the common people. Part of this style required access to ground level from two floors; in other words, it was built on a hill so both the basement and the first floor were on ground level. The other aspect is that the door is in the peak end of the house, as opposed to the drip side.

Revolutionary War soldier Lawrence Swart (1753–1841) purchased 230 acres, built the house, then lived there with his family until his death. The land was sold to Peter Collier and Jared Goodyear, who used this land to entice the railroad to come through Oneonta. In 1867, they sold the remaining 74 acres to Henry and Phoebe Adelaide (Smith) Wilcox for $9,000. The couple and their three children lived in the house for over one hundred years, with the last member of the Wilcox family, Merton, dying in 1970 at age ninety-two. In 1972 the City of Oneonta bought the Wilcox house with the remaining 14.7 acres of land and used it as the focal point for the city's 1976 Bicentennial Celebration.

Only the Swart and Wilcox families ever lived in the house, which is situated in a glorious rural setting surrounded by a small city. All the rooms in the house are included in the tour: early living area, front parlor, kitchen, milk room, pantry, and carriage shed; the second floor has two bedrooms and a large hall that was sometimes used as a bedroom.

When Phoebe Wilcox died in 1903 the house was frozen in time by her husband, Henry (1835–1912), and her two bachelor sons, Frederick (1867–1954) and Merton (1878–1970). Most of the original furnishings were displaced, but the house still has the original parlor set, stepback dresser, caned rocker, and ironstone dishes.

"While they respect the value of the authentic items in the house, they were mainly gifts from local families who used them daily, and as such, were meant to be touched and handled. They do this with care, but most of them are of sturdy materials that have lasted for one hundred to two hundred years, and will most likely be here for another hundred. So families do not have to be on edge worrying if their children touch something," says the program director about the museum's philosophy on the bygone articles it houses.

A couple of interesting artifacts that are viewable but not touchable were made by Phoebe's mother, Hannah (VanBuren) Smith: a cross-stitched sampler made in 1826 when she was twelve years old and a redwork coverlet made in 1890 when she was seventy-six years old. The 1826 sampler was found in a hope chest that was given to the Swart–Wilcox House in the 1990s.

The only other building on the property, which of course was a working farm back in the day, is the Swart corn crib filled with farm implements. In 2012 the corn crib was salvaged from the Peter Swart (one of Lawrence Swart's brothers) farm in Middleburgh, New York, after Hurricanes Irene and Lee washed it about a mile away from the original site. The corn crib, which fits the 1820 time period, was moved about forty-seven miles and restored by volunteers.

I went on a tour here a couple of years ago. My favorite part of the tour was learning how the Wilcox brothers heated the house until the last years it was lived in. They would cut down and limb a tree, then push the whole tree in the front door into the woodstove, which was about eighteen feet from the door, and keep feeding the tree into the woodstove as it burned. The tour guide told me that when they started to work on the house in 1972, absolutely everything was coated with soot and took a long time to clean.

Dr. Christopher Best House & Museum
1568 Clauverwie Rd., Middleburgh; (518) 827-7200;
drbesthouse.com; open Memorial Day through Labor Day;
admission free, donations appreciated

The Best House, as it is often referred to, is an amazing hidden treasure that sits right in the middle of Middleburgh. It is the only known exhibit of a nineteenth-century physician's office with its original equipment and furnishings in their original structure and location, and is enjoyable for all ages. Two doctors, father Christopher "Chris" Suits Best and his son Duncan, practiced medicine in the house for

a total of 107 years from 1884 to 1991. Chris practiced for fifty-eight years and Duncan fifty-six.

The Best House was built about 1884 and is an Italianate Victorian structure with a sweeping veranda. Behind the house is a large carriage house, which is open for tours on special occasions, and a tool shed. Of the five carriages and two sleighs in the carriage house, one is the carriage that Chris used to make house calls.

Christopher Best was born in 1852 in Fultonham to James and Elizabeth (Suits) Best. He studied medicine with Dr. John D. Wheeler (and later practiced with him) from 1870 to 1872 and graduated from the Eclectic Medical College in New York City in 1876. When he began practicing medicine on his own in 1883, his first patient was a child named Anthony W. Stevenson, who interestingly turned out to be his last patient as well. Christopher was the president of the Middleburgh Telephone Company (one of the first telephones is in a bathroom), Middleburgh Central School board of education, Schoharie County Red Cross Society, and Middleburgh & Schoharie Railroad, as well as Schoharie County coroner, an elder with St. Mark's Lutheran Church, and a Rotarian.

Christopher first married Laura Booth Scutt in 1877. She was born in 1857 to Henry Jr. and Matilda (Wainright) Scutt and died in 1889 of diabetes. They had one child, Blanche Suits, born in 1879, who married Emmett B. Vroman. His second wife was Ursula J. Leonard, daughter of Dr. Duncan Moore and Vashtie (McHench)

Leonard. They had three children: James, Emma, and Duncan. Christopher had to fill out a death certificate for his seven-year-old son James (1894–1901), who died of undulant fever caused by unpasteurized milk.

Duncan Leonard Best was born in 1903 in Middleburgh and died in 1991. He graduated from Union College in 1922 and Albany Medical College in 1930. Duncan married Winifred Wilkie. He went into practice with his father and was also a contract physician for the Civilian Conservation Corps camp and Middleburgh Central School, Schoharie County coroner, president of the Schoharie County Board of Health and Schoharie County Medical Society, and served in the US Army during World War II. Duncan Best bequeathed the house to the Middleburgh Library Association in 1991, and the first tour took place the following year. Duncan did not have any children, and his sister, Emma, who lived in the house until her death in 1982, never married, so the family line ended.

The following is a very small example of what you can view in the fourteen open rooms of the Best House. In the doctor's office are an apothecary, diathermy (electrically induced heat), hand-cranked centrifuge, trephine for drilling holes in the head, electrostatic machine for curing just about every malady imaginable, medical books, a stocked pharmacy, and a real human skull. The living area includes a 1920s kitchen with stocked shelves (the kitchen also has an operating table), three types of washing machines, a dumbwaiter, Victorian clothing, quilts, a horsehair chaise, a seashell curtain/room divider, a muddy putty jar/memory jar, a hand-cranked Victrola that still works, Duncan's bedroom as it was when he was a child, bathrooms with some of the first flush toilets (one still works), and a Civil War doctor's uniform that was worn by an uncle, George Henry Leonard. My favorites are a decorative newspaper or magazine holder that is built into the wall and a human hair wreath. All the artifacts in the house belonged to a member of the Best family, with the oldest being a book dated 1694. Sometimes tours of the basement are offered, where you can see thirty-plus-year-old canning jars filled with fruits and vegetables.

I volunteered as a docent here for a number of years and can assure visitors that they will be amazed.

Old Stone Fort Museum & Complex
145 Fort Rd., Schoharie; (518) 295-7192; theoldstonefort.org; open May through Oct; admission charged

The Fort, as most Schoharie County residents refer to it, was built as a Dutch Reform Church in 1772, became a fort during the Revolution, reverted back to a church until 1844, was an arsenal from 1857 to 1873 during and after the Civil War, then was given to Schoharie County and converted into a museum by the Schoharie County Historical Society in 1889. This is a complex of buildings, great for families to roam

around, that offers numerous periods in history pertaining to the Schoharie Valley, once called "The Breadbasket of the Revolution." Included in the price of admission are the Fort Museum and research library (owned by Schoharie County; the rest of the buildings are owned by the Schoharie County Historical Society), William Badgley Museum Annex built in 1972, Greek Revival Warner House circa 1830, John I. Jackson Law Office circa 1830, English-style Lacko Barn circa 1860, Oliver One-Room Schoolhouse and outhouse built in 1863, Hartmann's Dorf House circa 1786, Ingold-Schaeffer New World Dutch Barn circa 1780, a privy early 1900s, and a cemetery (not owned by the Schoharie Historical Society).

Builders of the church chiseled parishioners' names into some of the limestone blocks. Some of the parishioners' names, which are still visible today, were later chiseled out if it was felt they were Loyalists to Great Britain. This is the only surviving fort of the three forts utilized during the Revolution in the Schoharie Valley, and was called the Lower Fort. It was attacked on October 17, 1780, by a force of about eight hundred Loyalists/Tories and Indians and survived with only a cannon ball hole in a cornice at the rear of the building.

The Fort Museum still reflects the eclectic collecting and exhibit methods of the late Victorian era. Thousands of antiques and artifacts from times of war and peace are on exhibit in this "Cabinet of Curiosities," where you can discover examples of local geological formations such as "turtle rocks" and "clay buttons," hundreds of household items, toys, firearms, archaeological collections, and more. A famous firearm is the double-barreled rifle attributed to the legendary Revolutionary War sharpshooter Timothy Murphy. I think my favorite artifact is the "Kniskern Boxes" that were made by Johannes Kniskern in 1778 for his five-year-old twin daughters, Margreda and Elisabet Kniskern. The boxes, which are examples of German folk art, were separated for a number of years, then came back together at the Fort via different avenues.

One of the oldest fire engines, Deluge #1, sits in the fort. As the story goes, two fire engines, both built by Richard Newsham in England, arrived in New York City in December 1731 aboard the ship Beaver. The same story pertains to the Hayseeds fire engine that sits in the FASNY Museum of Firefighting in Hudson, New York. So it appears that the two oldest fire engines are still in NYS only fifty miles apart.

The Badgley building houses fine art, furniture, the "Age of Wood" exhibit, and a 1903 Rambler, the first automobile in the village. The Warner House displays the "Scribner Exhibit" of twentieth-century communication technology, including an outdoor movie projector. The Jackson Law Office, which was moved from Gilboa, houses materials related to Schoharie County law and government, including a 1925 voting machine. The Lacko Barn is currently used as a maintenance shop and storage. My favorite is the Oliver Schoolhouse because it was moved about twenty-five miles from where I live in Summit, and I have portrayed a schoolmarm there in the past. Children can get a feel for life as a scholar in the early 1900s by sitting at the desks and writing on the slates. The school was in operation in Summit until 1942. Hartmann's Dorf House was moved from about five miles away and is available for interior viewing by special arrangement. The Dutch Barn houses agricultural tools used in Schoharie County over the past three hundred years.

The Fort also has a well-stocked gift shop and offers special programs throughout the year.

CHAUTAUQUA–ALLEGANY

American Museum of Cutlery
9 Main St., Cattaraugus; (716) 257-9813; amcut.com; open year-round; admission free

The American Museum of Cutlery showcases more than 3,500 examples of knives, swords, axes, edged tools, and weapons. It is dedicated to preserving the stories of all cutlery manufacturers past and present.

The museum, which opened in 2005, relates the history and development of cutting instruments from pre-Columbian, colonial, Revolution, Civil War, and twentieth-century time periods, up to and including today's high art examples. Cutlery has been an important component of American history, and many cutlery companies originated in or around the Cattaraugus area in the late 1800s.

"Highlights that visitors are encouraged to look for when they visit are the knives of John Merritt, a World War II gunner; Dr. Rudolph Sandon's leaded-glass 'came' knife; Sergeant Charles W. Skemp's sword that was at his side as he served our country from 1863 through 1898; the John Jones knife; J.B.F. Champlin's vice #1; a

photo of the Windmill Road knife works; knives that were displayed at the Pan Am Exposition in 1901 in Buffalo, New York; a knife that was presented to Governor Theodore Roosevelt at a special dinner in 1899; the Ten Eyck Edge Tool Co. factory, located in Cattaraugus Village on South Street in 1883; one of the largest pocketknife hardware store box collections; the three knives made by Cattaraugus Cutlery during World War II, including an electrician's knife, a folding machete, and the 225Q; a whaling knife of the Charles W. Morgan; hand-forged blacksmith-made scissors; knives made to trade with the Indians; a Seneca Indian mask carver's knife owned by Calvin Kettle; an Indian "Crooked" knife; Revolutionary War naval cutlasses (a cutlass is a short sword with a slightly curved blade); War of 1812 cutlasses; Civil War Confederate Bowie

knives; French Napoleonic-era cutlasses used in the Confederacy; a pike used to protect Civil War cannon emplacements, and skinning knives," says the founder of the museum.

At the "Oh We Wish We Had a Bigger Museum Table," ask to see an adze, a broad-axe, a froe (tool used for splitting wood along the grain), a pit saw, a Chautauqua lake musky spear, a draw shave, and many other edged tools.

By appointment you can see the anvil and forging hammer, which were found in a barn in Cattaraugus, and photos of John Bottom, who came from Sheffield, England, to forge razors in Little Valley; an eighteenth-century Spanish dagger murder weapon used to kill Maria Monk in England in 1828; the developing history research project of the Ten Eyck Edge Tool Co. of Cattaraugus; a well-used World War II German Luftwaffe boot dagger, and the souvenir Russian sword of William "Bill" Erick of Arcade, who landed at Normandy and fought heroically through France, Belgium, Holland, and Germany and whose unit received a presidential citation; and historical items of Burrell Cutlery Co. of Ellicottville, New York, including the last straight razor made in the United States by one of America's best master cutlers.

The museum library, which is off-site, can also be visited by appointment.

Seneca-Iroquois National Museum
82 W. Hetzel St., Salamanca; (716) 945-1760; senecamuseum.org; open year-round; admission charged

Not only is this museum filled with an assortment of artifacts and displays from the seventeenth century to the present, even the floors, walls, and ceilings tell a story. The beginning of your walk tells the Seneca creation story that begins in the Sky World.

The Seneca-Iroquois National Museum collections consist of items from the six Hodinöhsö:ni' Nations: Seneca, Mohawk, Cayuga, Oneida, Onondaga, and Tuscarora, also known as the Iroquois.

All the signs in the museum, and even area road signs, are in both English and the Seneca language. Some of the gallery exhibits to walk through are "Distinct Community," "When It Began," "Milestones: What We Measure By," "On the Mothers Side," "All the Medicines," "Kinzua Dam" (the dam, built in the 1960s, claimed ten thousand acres of Allegany Reservation and displaced six hundred Seneca), and "Sovereignty: They Are Independent."

Items and displays I saw along the way during my visit included a milestone puzzle that tells the story of the thirteen Tadodaho leaders before European contact, a cradleboard for carrying a baby, current photos of families listing the clan they are a member of, a model pertaining to archaeological excavations along the Cowanesque River, arrowheads, antler carvings, basketry, ornate beadwork, an Iroquois beaded fan, a quilt honoring the Haudenosaunee women, French Jesuit rings and crucifixes from the 1600s to 1700s, a Seneca Nation Cattaraugus territory log cabin of the 1830s, the "Art of Tattoos" exhibit, an 1890 map of the Allegany Reservation of the Seneca Nation, Cattaraugus County, snowsnakes (a spear thrown down an icy trough for competition), a plaque for presidents of the Seneca Nation of Indians starting in 1848, Chief Cornplanter's tomahawk, and the history of World War II Code Talkers.

One of the displays that amazed me was about lacrosse. The sport is said to have been invented by Native Americans, who played the sport to honor their Creator. They currently have teams for under age nineteen ("U-19"), box lacrosse, men's Iroquois Nationals indoor and field, and Haudenosaunee women's lacrosse. The Iroquois Nationals became members of the Federation of International Lacrosse (FIL) in 1987 and are the only Native American team authorized to play a sport, any sport,

internationally. There are twenty-three teams in the FIL, and the Iroquois Nationals rank third in the world.

Scattered around the museum are handmade chairs and benches. The benches are etched with Hiawatha's belt and the eight clans. The seats are a welcome sight for a little rest and afford time to gaze at the displays or use as a photo op.

I asked the inventory manager at the admissions desk what his favorite aspect of the museum is, and he said the larger new facility, just opened in 2018, which allows for a lot more displays than the previous museum.

"The museum represents thousands of years of Native occupation in this region of Turtle Island. The museum is usually the first stop for many coming into Indian Country in the northeastern United States; as a result, every year they meet thousands of people from all walks of life from all over the globe. They are fortunate, and humbled, to serve as ambassadors. The Cornplanter Pipe-Tomahawk was returned to their community after being gone for 168 years. The pipe-tomahawk is special because it is an object from the birth of the United States and a symbol of the historical relationship between the Six Nations Confederacy and the United States. In the 1790s President George Washington gave the pipe-tomahawk to Seneca chief Cornplanter at the end of the negotiation of the Treaty of Canadaigua. Since then it was in two fires, purchased, sold, in a NYS museum, stolen, passed through many hands on the black market, in the New York State Museum, and finally returned to the Seneca-Iroquois National Museum in 2019," says the director.

The museum also houses the Seneca Nation Archives Department for the safe-keeping of historical documents. Call ahead if interested in researching the records.

Lucille Ball Desi Arnaz Museum & Center for Comedy
2 W. Third St., Jamestown; (716) 484-0800 and (877) 582-9326;
lucy-desi.com; open year-round; admission charged

This museum is probably best suited for the "Baby Boomer" generation, those born in the late 1940s and 1950s, as it will bring back fond memories of actors that you grew up with. The East Gallery mostly pertains to the *I Love Lucy* television show (1951–1957) and the West Gallery is more about Lucy and Desi's personal lives.

Lucille Desiree Ball (1911–1989) was born in Jamestown, New York, and grew up mostly in nearby Celoron. Desiderio "Desi" Alberto Arnaz (1917–1986) was born in Santiago de Cuba, and moved to Miami, Florida, in 1934 due to an upheaval in the Cuban government. They were married from 1940 to 1960 and had two children, Lucie and Desi Jr. They co-owned Desilu Productions from 1947 to 1962, then Lucy ran it on her own for a while.

The East Gallery has exhibit areas titled: "Radio Roots," "The Audition," "The New York Apartment," props & costumes, Fred & Ethel, the writers' room, Ricardos' Hollywood hotel room, backstage innovations, sound-stage model, "Live Like Lucy Bedroom Set," and "I Love Lucy Legacy," and a Vitameatavegamin photo op. (Vitameatavegamin was a fictitious health tonic imbibed by Lucy on a 1952 *I Love Lucy* episode.)

The West Gallery displays are "A Legacy of Laughter," "Story of Lucy and Desi," Lucy and Desi at Home," "Lucy in the Movies," "Lucy on TV," "Music of Desi Arnaz," "Lucy's Gold Mercedes," and "Lucy's Legacy Lives On."

Interesting artifacts that I found on my visit to the museum were Lucy's professor costume from 1951, Lucy's "Sally Sweet" costume 1951, Desi's "Cuban Pete" hat and congo drum, Lucy's ukulele, Ethel Mertz's shoes, the "women from Mars" belt, Lucy's saxophone 1952, "Queen of the Gypsies" necklace, Pepito the Clown's miniature bicycle and clown costume 1951, Fred Mertz's "Hippity Hoppity" costume, a moviola machine and the Three-Headed Monster (for editing), Lucy and Desi's stage chairs and portraits, Emmy awards, circus of the stars and cowgirl costumes, Lucy's Charlie Chaplin costume, Desi's office, Desi hosts *Saturday Night Live* 1975, and numerous *TV Guide* covers that featured Lucy.

I asked the young lady at the desk what her favorites were in the museum, and she picked the same two that I did. Lucy's gold 1972 Mercedes-Benz 280 SE was donated to the museum by her son-in-law Laurence Luckinbill, who had inherited the car from Lucy, when the museum opened in 1996. The other display that I found to be amazing was the twenty-four programs that Desilu Productions either filmed or produced besides *I Love Lucy*. One of the shows that Desilu produced that might not have come about was *Star Trek* (1966–1969). The Desilu board of directors did not like it, but Lucy did and pushed it through. As we all know now, Lucy made the right choice.

Jamestown is also home to five Lucy murals and statues, and her final resting place.

Dunkirk Lighthouse & Veterans Park Museum
1 Lighthouse Point Dr., Dunkirk; (716) 366-5050; dunkirklighthouse.com; open May to Oct; admission charged

The Dunkirk Light is also known as the Point Gratiot Light and has been a beacon for vessels on Lake Erie from 1826 to this day. Tour the museum that was the lighthouse keepers home, then walk up the cast-iron spiral staircase to the top of the sixty-one-foot-high lighthouse tower for a great view of the lake.

This is the site of the first shots fired in the War of 1812. The first lighthouse was established at Point Gratiot in 1826 and was lit by a lantern with thirteen lamps and reflectors fueled by whale oil. The second and current lighthouse, built of limestone, and attached High Victorian Gothic–style keepers home was built of brick in 1875. A third-order Fresnel lens was installed in the tower in 1857 and is one of only two still operating in NYS today. This beam of light has a range of twenty-seven miles.

Lake Erie, which also borders Pennsylvania, Ohio, and Michigan, is the twelfth-largest lake in the world, measuring 210 miles long and 57 miles wide with a maximum depth of 210 feet. It is the southernmost and shallowest lake of the Great Lakes.

"The second floor of the museum/house and the Coast Guard building are full of military artifacts, honoring all five branches of the service, from World War I, World War II, Korea, Vietnam, and Desert Storm, including a Mark 14 torpedo. Additional items of interest in the museum are a Victorian table setting, a plaque

dedicated to the lighthouse keepers from 1826 to 1960 (no keeper was needed after 1960 because the light was automated), an ornate wood-burning kitchen cookstove, a radio and switchboard, and military model airplanes," says the events coordinator.

On the property they have a thirty-ton "bottle" buoy that was originally part of the lighthouse system in Buffalo, an Armored Protected Vehicle (APV) used in Vietnam, a retired Coast Guard buoy tender (type of vessel used to maintain and replace navigational buoys) used on the Great Lakes, a Lyle cannon used by lighthouse stations to shoot a safety line for rescue operations, and a ship's bell dated 1823.

Ghost Hunts are offered at Dunkirk Lighthouse on occasional evenings due to potential paranormal activity. Some believe that the grounds are haunted by spirits of soldiers or keepers.

Alfred Ceramic Art Museum
1 Pine St., Alfred; (607) 871-2421; ceramicsmuseum.alfred.edu; open Feb through Dec; admission charged

There are very few museums focused solely on ceramics, but NYS is lucky enough to have one of them. The Alfred Ceramic Art Museum, located on the Alfred University Campus, houses nearly eight thousand ceramic objects. An easy way to find the museum is to look for the large Wave sculpture, by Eva Hild, out front.

The museum features collections of modern and contemporary American ceramic art, Asian and European porcelain, Chinese funerary jars, tomb scripture

from the Neolithic period, Roman and Byzantine lamps, Nigerian market pottery, and the Krevolin Collection of Pre-Columbian Pottery.

In 1900, Charles Fergus Binns was appointed as the founding director of the New York State College of Clay Working and Ceramics at Alfred University; thus the study of ceramic art and science was established as an educational focus at the university and has remained so for over a century. The permanent collection also includes works by international ceramic artists such as Rosanjin, Hamada, Leach, Cardew, and Rie and American ceramic art masters Ruth Duckworth, Ken Ferguson, Karen Karnes, Howard Kottler, Harrison MacIntosh, Ken Price, Peter Voulkos, Beatrice Wood, Betty Woodman, and Eva Zeisel, to name just a few.

"Visitors often enjoy the Master of Fine Arts (MFA) Collection, which now contains over seven hundred pieces, all created by MFA ceramic graduates. The collection began in the 1940s and grows by eight new pieces every year. This outstanding collection of graduate thesis work is unique in the world," says the operations and program manager.

The museum was designed by renowned American architect Michael McKinnell. According to the museum's director and curator: "Ceramic art offers an extraordinary window into the realm of human ingenuity and reveals clues to an understanding of art, architecture, industry, science, and engineering. Ceramic art tells the story of the creative mind and hand of humanity. Learning through the experience of viewing beautiful and unique objects is deeply rewarding. Visitors often remark that they had no idea ceramics had such an amazing history."

Normally the museum offers three different exhibitions per year, but it also has permanent large sculptures on display, such as the Madonna and Child by Waylande Gregory and Venus in a Half Shell by Philip Mayberry. Permanent collections are the Roger D. Corsaw, Colonel John R. Fox, David and Ann Shaner, Robert Turner, Visiting Artist, and George Wesp Collections.

Pioneer Oil Museum of New York
417 Main St., Bolivar; (585) 610-2038; pioneeroilmuseum.com; open Memorial Day through Sept; admission free, donations appreciated

I had no idea that NYS was involved in the oil industry, let alone laid claim to the first discovery of oil, by Seneca Indians, in North America, in Cuba, New York, in 1627. There are two museum venues: the Main Street location, an 1850s building that used to be the McEwen Brothers Oil field Supply Store and has served as the museum for forty-five years; and, within walking distance, the six-acre Hahn & Schaffner site, which includes seven buildings.

In 1865, Job Moses No. 1, located in Limestone, becomes New York's first successful oil well at seven barrels per day. A big strike at Rock City (southwest of Olean) in 1877 marked the start of NYS's first major oil field. The Triangle No. 1 near Allentown drilled in 1879, causing the town of Petrolia to spring up. In 1881, on the advice of a geologist, an investor group drilled a well on the Reading Farm in Richburg, New York. The well came in at seventy barrels on its first day, sparking the oil boom of 1881. Within days, hundreds of people began to flood into the valley, and within ten months there were between 4,500 to 5,000 people in Bolivar and 7,000 in Richburg. The first recovery period ran until the early 1920s when a new technology called "water flooding" was introduced. This new technology caused a secondary recovery in the area that peaked in the 1940s. The OPEC increase of oil prices in the 1970s caused new activity in the New York fields using new drilling and production technology. With the collapse of oil prices in 1986, production in the region went back into decline.

Galleries in the museum are the People Gallery, with a collection of photos of people working in the oil fields; the Sites and Scenes Gallery, with views around the Bolivar-Richburg area; the Tools and Devices Gallery, displaying tools used for the production of oil; and the Refinery Gallery, with pictures of the refinery that started operating in 1934. The museum is full of interesting artifacts. There is an authentic wagon "shooter's wagon" (a wagon used to "shoot" oil wells) from the early 1900s, which was driven from well to well by a shooter as he transported volatile nitroglycerin that was used to pour down a well (shoot) to create an explosion to help stimulate oil production deep below the surface; and a dynamite-making machine

dating to the early 1900s, a portable piece of equipment that was used to produce the large amount of dynamite needed in the local fields to shoot the oil wells (the dynamite was used to set off the nitro already placed in the hole). There's also a collection of large oil field engines and a collection of miniatures, including an oil lease, blacksmith, and sawmill; much of this collection, donated in 2018, was hand-made.

They also have a New York State Oil Producers' Association (NYSOPA) Wall of Fame that was established in 2005.

"Tourists are often shocked that there was such a large, vibrant oil/gas industry here beginning in the 1880s. They find out that this area was one of the wealthiest villages per capita (with more millionaires per capita) than any place in NYS from the 1920s until the 1960s or so. The total amount of oil produced in NYS from the 1870s through the present is about 245 million barrels," says one of the board members.

If in Bolivar the last week of June, check out their annual weeklong Pioneer Oil Days celebration.

Seward House Historic Museum
33 South St., Auburn; (315) 252-1283; sewardhouse.org;
open Feb through Dec for guided tours; admission charged

This museum was the historic home of William Henry Seward and his family. The museum director told me that 99.9 percent of the museum's collection is original to the family. It is as if they just left for the day.

William Seward (1801–1872) served as an NYS senator from 1831 to 1834, governor of New York from 1839 to 1842, a US senator from New York from 1849 to 1861, and US Secretary of State in the Lincoln and Johnson administrations from 1861 to 1869. He was one of the foremost politicians of nineteenth-century America. Seward married Frances Adeline Miller, who died June 1865 two months after she, William, and three of their children were attacked by an assassin on April 14, 1865, the same night that President Lincoln was assassinated. William was the intended victim of the organized attempt to take out Lincoln's administration, but he survived the numerous stab wounds to his face. His children also survived their knife wounds.

The museum houses an intact nineteenth-century collection of decorative items, books, fine art, furniture, textiles, glassware, silver, household items, and sculptures. A couple of the unique artifacts are an alabaster Buddha from Burma, acquired during Seward's 1871 world travels, and Fanny's Theater.

"The prominent position of Buddha in the dining room leads many of our guests to ask about the Seward family and their religion. Mrs. Seward grew up in a Quaker household and was deeply religious her entire life. Mr. Seward was not overly religious; however, he had a great deal of respect for people of all religions. Fanny's Theater: Fanny Seward (1844–1866) the youngest child, received this paper theater as a Christmas gift in 1858 when she was fourteen. It contains a wooden stage with holes for stage set pegs, three backdrops and seven forward props, and twenty-three figures (eighteen men and five women) that are between three and four inches high. Thanks to Fanny's remarkable record keeping in her diary, we know exactly when she received this gift and what she thought about it. She wrote, 'I woke very early and "rose with the sun" after lying awake for some time on coming into my little room I saw on a chair beside the chimney piece a large white box with a beautiful picture on the top, on opening it, I found a most beautiful little Theater, of paper, I knew at once that it was from my dearest mother and was delighted with it, dearest, best of mothers! how kind and thoughtful in the top of my stockings was a paper box in imitation of oak filled with paper actors for, as it announced, "The Mignon Theater,"

oh how very very neat and pretty." Considering it was a fourteen-year-old's toy, this charming theater is in impeccable condition, despite damage to one corner of the small box. But there is an explanation for that! In her January 2, 1859, diary entry, Fanny reported that she left the theater box somewhere that Belle, her puppy, could get his paws on it, and he chewed up the corner, as you can see in the picture," says the executive director.

Specialty tours by appointment only are Slavery to Emancipation, The Lincoln Tour: A Friendship that Shaped a Generation, (He)Art of the House, Speaking for Themselves: The Women of the Seward Family, Around the World with Mr. Seward, Mr. Seward's Junior Detective Tour, The Civil War Tour, Beyond the Garden Gate, The Seward Family in New York State, Haunted History Tours of Auburn (limited to the Halloween season), and Candlelight Tours (limited to the Christmas holiday season).

Ward O'Hara Agricultural & Country Living Museum
6880 E. Lake Rd., Auburn; (315) 252-7644; wardwoharaagriculturalmuseum.org; open year-round; admission free, donations accepted

This family-friendly museum, located in Emerson Park on the north shore of Owasaco Lake, is dedicated to the history of agricultural life in Cayuga County and surrounding counties.

Ward W. "The Story Teller" O'Hara (1918–1997) and his wife Ruth started collecting farm equipment in the mid-1900s, and when the collection grew beyond their ability to house it all, they looked for another site. They saw the 4-H pavilion at Emerson Park standing idle and approached the Cayuga County Legislature for permission to make it a country museum, which they did in May 1975.

Exhibit areas include a woodworker and blacksmith shop, creamery, general store, one-room schoolhouse, honey and dairy displays, a loom and textiles, feed and food processing equipment, a veterinary office, two kids' play areas, pottery, ice and hay harvesting equipment, lumber and saw equipment, "Power from a Treadwheel," a corn husker, "Golden Age of Industry," carriages, doll houses/miniatures, sleighs, oxen and plow, tractors, a colonial-style bedroom, and an early twentieth-century country kitchen with an attached parlor. Within the exhibit areas are numerous unique artifacts.

"The oldest item is a wooden shovel that was made in Denmark in the late 1600s, came to America with its owner, and had many years of use until it broke. The barn, full of antique tractors, includes a 1926 Model T Ford that was used by the founder of the museum, Ward O'Hara. We also have a 1927 Model T that is used for giving people rides on special events. In addition to the real tractors, we have a special collection of John Deere model tractors donated by a local collector. We have a bell that was used at the E.D. Clapp Company (the Clapp Company of Auburn made drop

forgings and also manufactured wagons). The bell was used so workers knew when it was time to get to work and when it was time to leave. The bell weighs one ton and reminds people of the Liberty Bell due to its size. There's a collection of miniature circus setups by the Circus Model Builders Club, and a collection of milk bottles from almost every dairy that operated in Auburn in the past," says a museum aide.

After visiting the museum, you can enjoy a picnic and go for a swim at the public beach.

Chemung County Historical Society & Museum
415 E. Water St., Elmira; (607) 734-4167; chemungvalleymuseum.org; open year-round; admission charged

This museum tells the story of Chemung County through interpretive exhibitions and also highlights some of its famous residents such as Mark Twain.

The front of the museum is housed in the Chemung Canal Bank. The bank was built of brick in 1833, combining elements of Greek Revival and Federal styles, and opened in 1834. A third floor was added in 1868, and it continued as a bank until 1920 when a new headquarters was built. The old bank housed law offices and apartments until the Chemung County Historical Society purchased it in 1982 and transformed it into a museum. This part of the museum houses permanent exhibits, and the addition in the back houses revolving exhibits.

Some of the interesting displays I found during my visit to the museum were the Langdon's summer home Quarry Farm where Mark Twain spent his summers, "The Inter-War Years 1920s," Chemung County town histories (this display changes every six months to highlight a different town), World War I, the Gilded Age following the Civil War, early Native American settlement, the Sullivan-Clinton Campaign during the Revolution, and the Confederate prisoner-of-war camp that was in Elmira. The camp started out as Camp Rathbun, a Union Army recruiting and training camp (1861–1864), then became a prison for over twelve thousand Confederate soldiers from July 1864 to July 1865. As a Confederate prison it was nicknamed "Helmira," where almost three thousand died, a staggering 24 percent death rate.

A few of the artifacts I noticed were a billiard table from the Langdon home (the Langdons were Mark Twain's in-laws), artifacts from Elmira Reformatory founder Zebulon Brockway, a Starr MI856 army revolver that was sold to raise funds for the Civil War, a Chemung Canal lock key, and Chemung County flag (the county was founded in 1836). One of the bank vaults holds a creative display of assorted artifacts.

Hands-on displays include headphones for a "History Through Song," with songs from Native American times through 1972; "Stereoscopes: The First 3D Pictures"; and a traced drawing of Mark Twain's signature table.

A highlight of the museum is the "Big Horn" mammoth tusk, from about eleven thousand years ago, which sits next to a display of fossils from the area. The Chemung River got its name when Native Americans found the tusk along its banks. The word Chemung is Algonquin for "place of the big horn."

An artifact that I have not seen anywhere else is the shell of an Aellograph barometer. It was made by Henry Clum, born in 1821 as Henrich Augustus Clum, an early meteorologist. Henry made numerous other styles of barometers throughout his life, but died in 1884 a rather poor man.

The Booth Library is also open year-round for genealogical and historical research of the Chemung Valley.

Mark Twain Trolley Tours leave from the museum, on the hour, during July and August; call ahead for information. Also available is a Mark Twain in Elmira cell phone audio tour. Twain's real name was Samuel Langhorne Clemens (1835–1910).

National Soaring Museum
51 Soaring Hill Dr., Elmira; (607) 734-3128; soaringmuseum.org; open year-round; admission charged

There are only two soaring museums in the United States that are focused on motorless flight. Elmira is often regarded as the "Soaring Capital of America," in part because of soaring's central role for ninety years in the social and economic history of the region.

The Federal Aviation Administration's definition of an aircraft without an engine is a glider. The National Soaring Museum refers to them as "sailplanes," a term dating back to the 1930s, because they are meant to soar (remain aloft) on upward-moving air currents (the most common being thermals and ridge lift).

On July 2, 1930, the first sailplane flight took place in Elmira when Jack O'Meara flew his Baker McMillan Cadet II for one hour and thirty-eight minutes. This sailplane, which is at the museum, has a wingspan of 37.5 feet, is 19 feet long, and an empty weight of 239 pounds. The Baker McMillan Cadet flew again at the first national soaring contest, which took place in September 1930.

The first thirteen national soaring contests were held here between the years 1930 and 1947. A contributor to the soaring effort was Schweizer Aircraft Corporation, of Elmira, which produced half of all American sailplanes starting in 1930. In 1934, Chemung County purchased the land that was to become Harris Hill and the site for the museum. At the outbreak of World War II, Elmira was also the first site chosen to develop a glider program and train pilots for the war effort. Soaring contests that took place in the 1950s led to the idea of starting a soaring museum, which the Soaring Society of America did in 1969. Regional, national, and international sailplane contests and meets have continued through the years in the summer.

"I enjoy the sheer beauty of the location and am moved by the historic presence of American pioneer soaring pilots, showcased at the museum, who flew off Harris Hill. I have often heard tourists say, 'Wow, there's so much more to see here than I expected,'" says the director.

The museum's collection of thirty-two gliders date from the late 1890s to 1970s. Some of the gliders I noticed on my visit to the museum were a 1898 Chanute hang glider, 1938 Deutsche Forschungsanstait fur Segelflug (DFS) Olympia Meise, 1935 Goppingen Wolf I, World War II Waco CG-4A troop and cargo glider, 1941

Bowlus BTS-100, 1948 Ross-Johnson RJ-5, 1946 Kursawe Kirby Gull II, 1937 RS-1 Zanonia, 1975 Schreder HP-18, and 1942 Schweizer SGS 2-12.

Non-flying artifacts that I noticed were a trophy case, old baragraphs (used to record atmospheric pressure), a circa 1930 shock cord launch diorama, a 1937 E. Paul du Pont winch truck (used to launch sailplanes), and 150 model sailplanes. You can also sit in the cockpit of a Schweizer SGS 1-34 for a photo op.

Harris Hill Soaring Corporation offers sailplane rides from April through October. The long runway sits right in front of the museum. As you drive up to the museum, you go through Harris Hill Amusement Park, with lots of kid things to do in the summer.

The 1890 House Museum
37 Tompkins St., Cortland; (607) 756-7551; the1890house.org; open year-round; admission charged

Step back in time to nineteenth-century Cortland and learn about the Wickwire family, their servants, and the employees of their Wickwire Wire Mills Factory. The museum got its name because Chester Wickwire and his family moved into their limestone Gothic Revival, thirty-room mansion in 1890.

"The architecture of the museum was inspired by the home of James Bailey of Barnum & Bailey Circus. (The Bailey home still stands at 10 St. Nicholas Pl., New York City.) Chester Wickwire contracted Samuel B. Reed, the architect of James Bailey's home, to build a mirror image of the home in Cortland. The house was completed in a matter of eighteen months," says the associate director.

Chester Franklin Wickwire (1843–1910) first opened a hardware store in 1865, then after reconfiguring a carpet loom to weave wire, he closed his hardware store, partnered with his brother Theodore (1851–1926), and started producing wire cloth in 1876. Chester developed useful products such as horse muzzles, seed spreaders, window screens to keep insects out, coal sieves, and popcorn poppers. His son Charles, whose red mansion sits next to the 1890 mansion, took over the company until his death in 1956. The youngest son, Frederic (1883–1929), also worked at the family business and moved into the family home in 1923. The last Wickwire to live in the mansion was Frederic's wife, Marion (1888–1973). It became a museum two years after her death.

"Chester Wickwire's heritage can be traced back to the Norman conquest when William the Conqueror defeated Harold, son of Edward the Confessor, at the battle of Hastings in AD 1066. In 1675, John Wickware emigrated to New London, Connecticut. He died in 1712 and his will was offered for probate at the Probate Court where the clerk of the court entered his name as John Wickwire. Thus the name 'Wickwire' was born, 131 years before the birth of Chester Wickwire," says the associate director.

"Chester was very fond of racehorses and invested large sums in the purchase and upkeep of fine horses to race. Their trotters raced in the central New York circuits, and their carriage horses supported superior accouterments. Winnie Wick was the most famous of the Wickwires' racers, and could trot a mile in under two minutes twenty seconds. She successfully completed the eastern circuit in 1884. In 1885, Chester sold her for $2,000. Chester also kept a cow behind his house and would at times harness the cow to pull his carriages."

My first thought when I entered the Wickwire home was elegance and then some. On the first floor is an entrance hall with a unique alcove under the stairs with bench seats and a fireplace, the east parlor, the gold parlor (which Marie Antoinette would have fit right into), the music room, a sun parlor and fernery with an exquisite stained-glass ceiling, library, dining room, and kitchen. The second floor has display cases with examples of what the Wickwire Company made, a Victorian hair wreath, a master bedroom with a telephone attached to the wall, a large bathroom with a unique shower, a morning room often used as a casual reception room, the children's bedroom, and servants' quarters. On the third floor is a ballroom with a billiard table and piano, which was thought to have partitions in the past to make a smoking and card room.

Tompkins Street is nice to drive along if you like big, old, elegant houses.

Central New York History Center
4386 US Rte. 11, Cortland; (607) 299-4185; cnylivinghistory.org; open year-round; admission charged

Truly a museum for the whole family, the Central New York (CNY) History Center opened in 2012 in a repurposed old shopping center. Sometimes it is hard to get guys and kids interested in visiting a museum, but you will have no problem with this one, as it has trucks, tractors, model trains, and military memorabilia.

There are three museums in one here—Homeville, Brockway Museum, and Tractors of Yesteryear—and a gift shop.

Homeville was Kenneth "Ken" M. Eaton's (1926–2006) personal museum and consists mostly of military, railroad, and Cortland County heirlooms. Ken bought a Civil War rifle as a teenager and from there kept collecting and collecting artifacts until he had to buy another house for his collections, then opened his own museum in 1976. When you enter the room there is a large (very large) operational model train set up, a model train display, Erie Lackawanna Railway artifacts, and a replica of the front of a locomotive. A fraction of the rest of the displays I noted were the Cortland baseball team, women's suffrage, Smith Corona Marchant company, a wide assortment of Civil War artifacts and uniforms, military uniforms from assorted years, American flags listing when stars for states were added to the flag, a 1912 Ford ambulance, a World War I trench replica, German military paraphernalia, a World War II British BSA Airborne folding bicycle, local fire departments, police history, the Cortland Harness & Carriage Goods Co., and an assortment of rifles. One of the tour guides' favorites is an 1861 Enfield London Armory Civil War rifle used by George H. Fredenburg.

Brockway Motor Company was a builder of custom heavy-duty trucks in Cortland from 1912 to 1977. Brockway Carriage Works was founded by William Brockway in 1875, and his son George started manufacturing trucks in 1909. Brockway was purchased by Mack Trucks Inc. in 1956. Most of the fourteen or so trucks on display are loaned to the museum by their owners, so the exhibit is always changing. One of the trucks is a 1925 Brockway Fire Truck that four guys brought seventeen thousand miles to Cortland from Argentina during the years 1958 to 1960. Also on the first floor with the trucks is an air brake system mounted on a board so you can see exactly how a truck is able to stop. Look up toward the second floor to see the 1883 Cortland City Clock that was in the 2006 Parker Building fire and amazingly restored. On the second floor is the history of Brockway, some Brockway carriages, a mock Brockway office, and memorabilia. "Brockway was very good at making tchotchkes to promote their brand," says the director, who gave me my private tour.

Just across the parking lot is the Tractors of Yesteryear (TOYS) barn with about a dozen antique tractors, agricultural implements, tools, and a "family life of old" room. Tour guide favorites include the 1937 John Deere model BR and a player piano that kids think a ghost is playing.

National Warplane Museum
3489 Big Tree Ln., Geneseo; (585) 243-2100;
nationalwarplanemuseum.com; open year-round; admission charged

The National Warplane Museum is a hands-on site where all ages can sit in and crawl around airplanes that flew during World War II, the Korean War, and the Vietnam War. If you are so inclined, you can even book a flight on some of the airplanes, for an additional fee.

The all-volunteer staff of the museum, which was founded in 1994, are dedicated to restoring, repairing, flying, and displaying vintage military aircraft and equipment, and honoring the men and women who served our country at home and abroad. Some of the planes ("warbirds") on-site are flying, some do not fly anymore, and some are in the midst of repairs. Saturdays are a good day to visit if you are interested in chatting with some of the mechanics while they work on planes.

The premier plane is the C-47 "Whiskey 7," which is truly a World War II veteran and one of the planes you can book a ride on. This aircraft originally served with the 12th Air Force in the Mediterranean Theater in 1943 and the 9th Air Force in England from 1944 to 1945 as part of the 316th Troop Carrier Group. It was one of the lead aircraft of the first strike of the D-Day invasion on June 6, 1944, over Ste. Mere Eglise, Normandy. It transported paratroopers for the 82nd Airborne Division

as part of Operation Neptune. Flak was very heavy during these missions, but this C-47 managed to survive it all. The plane was flown to Normandy in 2014 for the seventieth anniversary of the D-Day invasion.

Some of the rest of the fleet on display include a C-45 flying Beechcraft, C-130A, Antonov AN-2 (also called a colt), Beechcraft US 45, Fairchild C-119, B-23 Dragon (one of only thirty-eight built), a second C-47, AT-6 trainer, L-Birds (L for Liason) two-seaters, and Aeronca L-16A.

The visitor center displays an assortment of authentic World War II uniforms including women's and children's, a huge collection of model airplanes, and a very nice D-Day diorama. A tour guide told me visitors often light up when they see the Link Trainer (a type of flight simulator), another flight simulator with both the mock airplane and the instructor's table with all the equipment.

The National Warplane Museum Airshow, which takes place in July, is sometimes called the "Greatest Show on Turf" because organizers use a five-thousand-foot grass air strip/runway located on the grounds of the Geneseo Airport. During the show you can check out all the planes and talk to the pilots.

As mentioned, the museum is open year-round, but the hangar is chilly in the winter.

Livingston County Historical Society Museum
30 Center St., Geneseo; (585) 243-9147;
livingstonhistoricalsociety.com; open May through Dec;
admission free, donations appreciated

This museum houses two hundred years of stories and collections from seventeen towns in Livingston County, each unique and rich in history. The museum is housed in the former District #5 Cobblestone Schoolhouse, which opened in 1838, was closed to students in 1932, then immediately repurposed as a museum. Also on the museum grounds is the Willard Hose House circa 1890, moved here in 1989.

"The museum houses a section of the famous Big Tree, which grew strong during the time that Native Americans lived in the Genesee Valley and before the signing of the Big Tree Treaty in 1797. For hundreds of years, this massive oak tree stood on the bank of the Genesee River two miles west of the museum. It survived fire and flood, conquest and greed to become an icon of the Genesee Valley and a meaningful landmark for the people who lived here. Today, as an organic artifact, an ecofact, the Big Tree speaks to us of forgotten landscapes and dares us to solve mysteries: Why did these oaks grow so big, and why did an oak savanna exist where there should have been a forest? As a cultural icon, the Big Tree evokes strong memories of invaluable land—and conflicting values. It invites us to reimagine a place we thought we knew and rediscover the many people who planted roots here and called the Genesee Valley home," says the museum administrator.

Other exhibit areas include "Always About the Land," which tells a story of Livingston County from pre-European settlement to the present day by incorporating nine artifacts, a large artist-created background mural of the Livingston County countryside, and a narrative graphic rail connecting a visitor with a meaningful county identity and sense of place. "Groveland Shakers 1826–1892" describes the community that settled in Groveland, New York. Shakers is the common name for the religious denomination, the United Society of Believers in Christ's Second Appearing. The Home and Hearth room displays mostly nineteenth-century objects commonly used for cooking, cleaning, and sewing. "Salt Mining in the Genesee Valley" displays images, documents, and artifacts from the mining industries that began in 1878. The "Schoolhouse Days" exhibit presents visual images and artifacts representing education in Livingston County, primarily during the years 1820 to 1932. The "World War I" exhibit examines this war from world, national, and local perspectives and features a digital collection of local photographs. The "Our Towns: The History of Livingston County in 25 Objects" exhibit will introduce you to a handful of the stories that contribute to the mosaic of life in Livingston County.

Also on display are the Wadsworth family coach, purchased in 1873; a Civil War drum and a thirty-four-star hand-embroidered US flag of the Wadsworth

Regiment; Native American objects, including a mortar and pestle; Big Tree paintings; and a folk art weathervane.

Susan B. Anthony Museum & House
**17 Madison St., Rochester; (585) 235-6124; susanb.org;
open year-round for guided tours; admission charged**

Susan B. Anthony was involved in the abolition of slavery, suffrage, education reform, labor reform, and temperance throughout her life.

Susan Brownell Anthony was born in 1820 in Adams, Massachusetts, then moved to Rochester with her family in 1845. She was active in the antislavery and temperance movements and the fight for women's rights and suffrage right up until

her death in 1906 following her "Failure Is Impossible" speech given in Baltimore. Fourteen years after Susan B. Anthony's death, the 19th Amendment was passed, which gave women the right to vote.

The two-story, twelve-room, brick Italianate-style house that became Anthony's home in 1865 was built in 1859. In 1892 she made the house the headquarters of the National American Women's Suffrage Association, as she had become the group's president, and in 1894 it became public offices for the New York State Constitutional Campaign. The house was owned by assorted families until 1945 when the Rochester Federation of Women's Clubs raised $8,500 to buy it.

The restoration of the house back to the time period that Anthony lived there has been an ongoing project that began in 1998. The exterior has been refurbished, and the interior restoration includes installing historic-reproduction wallpaper; replicating the original faux-grain painting on doors, floors, and windows; and replacing late twentieth-century light fixtures with modern equivalents of the original gas lights.

An interesting, funny tidbit published in the February 6, 1879, *Gilboa Monitor* read: "The lecture, by Susan B. Anthony, at Cobleskill, was a 'fizzle' financially." Cobleskill is in Schoharie County, New York, which is about a three-hour drive from Rochester.

I went to this museum in 1995, and unbeknownst to me there was some kind of celebration about to take place. When I walked up to the door, someone asked if I was with the press and I told them, "No, I'm from Summit, Schoharie County, New York, and just want to tour the house." So I got a special and free tour.

George Eastman House and the International Museum of Photography and Film
900 East Ave., Rochester; (585)327-4800; eastman.org; open year-round; admission charged

"The George Eastman Museum has something for everyone. For those that love history we have the restored home of Eastman Kodak Company founder George Eastman and exhibits that tell the story of how he made photography simple and easy enough for everyone to take pictures. For those that love the outdoors we have the opportunity to stroll and photograph in three different formal gardens that surround Eastman's Colonial Revival-style home, and for those that love photography, cameras, and movies we have exhibits and displays that inform and entertain all age levels of visitors. Visitors are often 'wowed' by the fact that there are modern photography galleries built onto the historic home of George Eastman. The museum also has two theaters, a cafe, and a nice gift shop, so if you like to shop there is something for you too," says the curator.

George Eastman was born in 1854 in Waterville, New York, and moved to Rochester with his parents and two older sisters in 1860. Throughout his adult life he was an entrepreneur, a philanthropist (he donated $100 million dollars during his lifetime), and the pioneer of popular photography and motion picture film. The Eastman mansion that you visit is the same home he had built and lived in until his death in 1932.

Areas to visit are the Main Galleries, with exhibitions of photography and moving images from those mediums' beginnings to today; the Project Gallery, which displays contemporary works and thematic projects; the History of Photography Gallery, a rotating installation of photographs and cameras from the museum's collections; the historic mansion where you can explore the restored rooms of this National Historic Landmark, built between 1902 and 1905, and see how George Eastman lived; the Second Floor Galleries, which trace the evolution of early photographic technology through cameras from the collection; and the gardens for touring at your own pace.

A couple of interesting aspects of the museum are an Aeolian pipe organ and hidden safes. George Eastman had a huge Aeolian pipe organ installed in his home in 1905, when he moved in. Over the years he had it expanded to the point where pipes surrounded his entire conservatory. He was one of the first to have a surround sound system in his home. Today visitors enjoy listening to local organists perform on the restored instrument, and when an organist is not available organ rolls can be played for their enjoyment. Hidden wall safes were installed to store Eastman's china, crystal, and silver and his important papers. One safe is in the dining room hidden behind oak doors, and the other is on the second floor near the staircase.

Erie Canal Museum
318 Erie Blvd. E., Syracuse; (315) 471-0593; eriecanalmuseum.org; open year-round; admission charged

Go back in time to the early and mid-1800s and explore life in an Erie Canal town. The original Erie Canal was built between 1817 and 1825 and stretched 363 miles from Albany to Buffalo. It was sometimes called "Clinton's Folly" because some thought New York governor DeWitt Clinton was crazy for building it.

Permanent exhibits and spaces at the museum include "The Erie Canal Made New York," which details the history and construction of the canal, from earliest conception to the modern barge canal system; the Weighlock Building, built in 1850, which contains exhibits pertaining to the financing of the canal, the function and operation of the Syracuse Weighlock, and Syracuse-specific topics such as folk musician Elizabeth "Libba" Cotten; the Weigh Chamber, which contains the sixty-five-foot-tall Frank Buchanan Thomson, a full-size replica line boat that visitors can explore; second-floor exhibits devoted to re-creating life in a canal town, with examples of an era tavern, general store, and theater, plus an exhibit about Onondaga pottery/Syracuse china; a children's area that is special for the youngest visitors, where they can read books about the canal, play with traditional toys, try on historical clothing, or put on a puppet show; murals depicting life on the canal, canal businesses, elevation changes along the canal, and the operation of a lock; the Locktender's Garden, a re-creation of a Victorian-era canal-side garden, with plants

authentic to the period; and artwork that includes *Madonna of the Canal* by Elizabeth Leader (2015) and *Clinton Square, circa 1864* by Mark Topp (1993).

The collections of the Erie Canal Museum consist of a wide variety of items reflecting the material culture of the nineteenth and early twentieth centuries in Upstate New York. These collections include objects such as a diving helmet and suit used for repairing the canal underwater; prints, sketches, drawings, and paintings; photographs and glass plate negatives; rare books; and miscellaneous maps, plans, receipts, and other manuscript and archival material.

I found information about the weighlock in the March 5, 1903, *Evening Herald*, Syracuse: "Five thousand dollars are being expended in repairs on the weighlock and when the work is done the interior of the building will be entirely new. The weighlock building was built about 1850, and is as substantial today as it was when built. The weighlock is now a misnomer for it has not been used as a weighlock in about twenty-five years since the abolition of canal tolls. It is now a canal office. Until the present repairs were made the Syracuse weighlock and that at Troy were the only ones still intact as weighlocks, where boats could be weighed. Now the big scales have been removed."

Stickley Museum
300 Orchard St., Fayetteville; (315) 637-2278; stickley.com/museum; open year-round; admission free

Over a century of some of America's best-made furniture is housed at the Stickley Museum. The eight-thousand-square-foot exhibit gallery contains furniture and accessories from the earliest days of Stickley up to the present, as well as a variety of images and archival documents illustrating the company's journey.

"One thing people don't realize about the Stickley Museum is that we are located in the former L. & J. G. Stickley (brothers Leopold and John George Stickley) factory, which is now home to the museum and the Fayetteville Free Library. Many pieces on display, and those found downstairs in the library, were made in this building," says the director.

The Stickley story began with three words: Als Ik Kan—"to the best of my ability." This old Flemish craftsman's phrase has been the guiding principle of Stickley since 1900. Five Stickley brothers, whose parents emigrated from Germany, were all involved in furniture-making, sometimes together and sometimes individually in a few states. Gustav Stickley (1858–1942) formed Stickley Brothers & Company in 1883 with brothers Charles (1860–1927) and Albert (1863–1928), then he and brother Leopold (1869–1957) burst into international prominence in the early twentieth century with their Mission Oak designs. Stickley Brothers used solid construction, what-you-see-is-what-you-get joinery, and the highest quality woods.

Gustav also started publishing *The Craftsman* magazine in 1901, which helped promote his American Arts and Crafts furniture.

Early designers who collaborated with Gustav and Leopold were Henry Wilkinson, Lamont Warner, Louise Shrimpton, Peter Hansen, and Harvey Ellis. There is still a Harvey Ellis collection today.

Following Leopold's death in 1957, his wife Louise ran the company until 1974, when the Stickley legacy was passed on to the Audi family and continues to this day under their tutelage and a new name, Stickley, Audi & Company.

Ontario County Historical Museum
**55 N. Main St., Canandaigua; (585) 394-4975; ochs.org;
open year-round; admission free**

It is pretty amazing to find a museum that was built specifically as a museum and public library over one hundred years ago. This Georgian Revival–style building, designed by famed architect Claude Fayette Bragdon (1866–1946), was built in 1914, at the beginning of World War I, with monies raised by the Canandaigua community.

"My favorite aspect of the museum is the architecture of the building and the fact that it is in the city historic district, and is an active cultural center in our county for art and history. Tourists are often amazed that the building was designed by such a renowned architect, a contemporary of the architect Frank Lloyd Wright," says the executive director.

The museum offers rotating exhibits and monthly educational programs pertaining to the origins of western New York. There are three exhibit galleries, including the "Pioneer Kitchen," which was built as such in 1914. The Ontario County Historical Society began to occupy the whole building in 1972 when the Wood Library Association public library relocated.

The object collection includes furniture, clothing, agricultural equipment, household items, medical artifacts, military artifacts, fine artwork, toys, and Native American items. Some of the artifacts you might see are a coffee pot made by Lisk Manufacturing Company of Canandaigua, a Dionne Quintuplets doll set circa 1935, a studio camera circa 1855, a sampler made in 1824 by Asenath Ferre of Bristol, New York, the leg irons worn by John Kelly of Geneva, New York, in 1889, a nineteenth-century electrotherapy machine for nervous diseases, artwork by Erma Hewitt of West Bloomfield, an American flag quilt, an oil painting of Joshua Stearns dated 1843, a cloak circa 1785 to 1795, and a silver Peace Medal etched with a Native American with pipe and George Washington dated 1792.

The museum also houses a local history archives and library for researchers and a book shop where local history books can be purchased.

Phelps Community Historical Society Museum
**66 Main St., Phelps; (315) 548-4940; phelpsny.com;
open year-round; admission free**

A rare, two-story privy/outhouse is the highlight of the Howe House Museum, home to the Phelps Community Historical Society, built of brick in 1869 in the Second Empire style. Originally this was the home of Dr. John Quincy Howe, who

besides being a doctor was a successful malt mill owner. The society also owns and shows, on a limited basis, the Country Lawyer's Office, built about 1835.

Dr. John Quincy Howe (1818–1891) married Nancy Amelia Giffith (1827–1914) on March 4, 1843, and they had seven children that included two sets of twins. The last set of twins were boys, Pearl and William, who both became doctors. Pearl moved to the Midwest in about 1900 and William remained at the Howe homestead. William Augusta Howe (1862–1940) married Elizabeth M. Partridge (1872–1955), and they had at least three children. William practiced medicine for twenty years in Phelps, became part of the NYS Health Department's communicable disease division in 1909 and supervisor of health education in NYS schools in 1915, and organized the American Association of School Physicians in 1927.

"The Howe House Museum home collections include more than four thousand items, mostly those that have a connection with Phelps and its history, such as being made here or belonging to a local family. In addition to business, farm, and household items, there are over one hundred scrapbooks containing births, marriages, and deaths of the people of Phelps, as well as happenings that occurred," says the director.

The Howe House, which sports a mansard roof, offers tours through a parlor room, a sauerkraut room, a military room, and a children's room. Phelps was known as the "Sauerkraut Capital of the World" from the early 1900s until 1985 and started having annual sauerkraut festivals starting in 1967.

There are only about a dozen two-story privies left in the United States, and this one is thought to be the only brick privy. It is attached to the house and offers provisions for three occupants upstairs and three downstairs. At ground level is a wooden tray that slides out for cleaning. I would not want that cleaning job.

The Country Lawyer's Office, a one-story redbrick building, became well known after a best-selling novel, *The Country Lawyer*, was written in 1939 by Bellamy Partridge. The book was about Bellamy's father, Samuel Selden Partridge (1839–1913), who practiced law for about forty years in this building.

Schuyler County Historical Society
108 N. Catharine St./Rte. 14, Montour Falls; (607) 535-9741; schuylerhistory.org; open year-round; admission free, donations appreciated

The Schuyler County Historical Society's flagship facility is the Brick Tavern Museum. The Federal-style tavern is the oldest brick structure in Schuyler County, built in 1828. It was built as a tavern on the stagecoach route and has also been a Select School for Boys, a boardinghouse, and home to Dr. Charles D. Clawson, who ran the nearby Bethesda Sanitarium. After Dr. Clawson's death the building continued as a family home until his grandson, the late Charles Lattin, sold it to the Society

in 1974. One of the characteristics that remains from its days as a tavern are two tall closets that flank the front door. These closets, it is believed, were where tavern visitors were required to leave their guns when they entered. The tavern museum features the "Music in the Foyer" exhibit; a Victorian parlor, research library, toy room, and gift shop; and Native American, veterans, medical, industry, clothing, fiber arts, and Watkins Glen State Park displays.

"A recent addition to the Schuyler County Historical Society's property is the Wickham Rural Life Center, which celebrates agriculture and home life in Schuyler County. The building features a wide array of tools, a kitchen setting with a dual wood-gas stove, an exhibit about the history of the county's world-renowned wine industry, and a salute to the dairies of the past. Among the oddities: a dog-powered treadmill that provided the energy to a butter churn," says the executive director.

The Society also is proud of its Lee School Museum, a one-room schoolhouse located just south of the village line on Route 14. The Lee School was built in 1884, and is furnished exactly as it was in the early twentieth century. The Lee School is open for special events twice a year and by appointment at any time. Visiting school students are enchanted by the wooden desks and potbellied stove, while adults may be more fascinated by the antique world globe.

Montour Falls was originally called Catharine's Landing after Queen Catharine Montour, a prominent Iroquois leader, then in 1836 it was incorporated as the Village of Havana and finally became Montour Falls in 1893. The twenty-ninth governor of NYS was David Bennett Hill, who was born in Havana/Montour Falls in 1843. He served two terms, from 1885 to 1892, and died in 1910.

International Motor Racing Research Center
**610 S. Decatur St., Watkins Glen; (607) 535-9044;
racingarchives.org; open year-round; admission free**

Learn about the history of the Grand Prix race that began in 1948 and grab a map to drive the original course.

"A visit to the International Motor Racing Research Center is a 'step back' into the evolution of motor racing. The photos, programs, films, posters, and other memorabilia that fill the shelves here instantly bring back memories of an earlier era. A time when drivers seemed 'larger than life,' race cars were designed by humans not computers, and the corporate world had not invaded the sport to the degree it has today. For the fan, motor racing is a sensory experience on so many levels. The shape and color of the cars flashing by . . . the magnificent sound of the engines . . . the odor of racing fuel wafting through the air . . . even the smell of burgers and hot dogs at the concession stand . . . it's an all-encompassing experience. I am reminded of a lifetime of such memories each time I walk in here, and that is my favorite aspect of the center. For my part, as the visitor services coordinator, if we could only recreate the aroma of burgers mixed with the smell of racing fuel, the place would be perfect! Most of our visitors are unaware that the small but bustling village of Watkins Glen, New York, was the birthplace of post-World War II road racing in the United States. On a chilly October day in 1948, road racing came back to the United States as brave, daring men raced around a 6.6-mile course of public roads circling the State Park and running through the streets of the village. Mention 'The Glen' to race fans in the United States and around the world and they will instantly know what you are talking about," says the visitor services/outreach coordinator.

One interesting artifact is a handwritten letter by British Formula One racing driver Stirling Moss (1929–2020) on Glen Motor Court stationery to the organizers of the inaugural Mexican Grand Prix (scheduled for November 26, 1961) stipulating his demands to compete. The demands, in part, read: "Payment of $7500 US or Sterling equivalent . . . payment to be in escrow in London or Nassau, Bahamas by Oct. 14 and agreeing that the money was to be paid regardless of revolution, kidnapping, or any other cancellation or postponement of the event. The only reason the money would not be payable would be if Stirling chooses not to compete or was ill."

Another item is a competition license issued for a "Fred Wheeler" on August 21, 1964, only the photo on the license is Stirling Moss! Renowned motor racing historians Karl Ludvigsen and Doug Nye (both members of the IMRRC's Historians Council) cannot explain why Moss would have filed for a license under an assumed name. The date of issue was two years after his career-ending crash

while racing and two years before he became more visible in the United States by promoting the Can-Am series.

The Werner Winter Collection is a collection of programs, magazines, and other memorabilia dating back to 1927 from the legendary German racetrack, the Nur-burgring (the Ring). In its early configuration, the Ring wound dramatically for more than seventeen miles through the Eifel forests and mountains. With elevations of more than one thousand feet and 174 corners, this was a track for only the brave and talented. The great Formula One champion, Niki Lauda, was almost killed here in 1976. Arguably one of the most famous racecourses in the world, looking through the almost fifty years of programs dramatically chronicles eras of racing when drivers were truly "larger than life."

The Joseph Stalk Collection of scrapbooks, lovingly compiled by Mr. Stalk, tells the story of sprint and midget car racing on the short tracks of the Northeast in the mid- to late 1940s. Sprint and midget racing is a uniquely American form of racing. The photos and programs in this collection are simply wonderful and take you back to an earlier era of racing. Sprint and midget car racing is tremendously popular today, but it's great to be able to take a look back to this earlier era.

My husband and I camped out in the middle of this track in the 1970s, while a race was taking place. What fun it was!

The National Memorial Day Museum
35 E. Main St., Waterloo; (315) 539-9611; wlhs-ny.com; open Memorial Day through Labor Day; admission free

The Memorial Day Museum strives to educate visitors on the founding of Memorial Day and the service/sacrifice of America's veterans.

Decoration Day was the original name for Memorial Day, and it began after the Civil War ended. In 1865 Henry Carter Welles (1821–1868), of Waterloo, started to talk about honoring the dead veterans, and after getting together with General John B. Murray the next year, the idea was brought to fruition. People decorated the graves of the war dead and recognized their service in the American armed forces during a village-wide celebration, held on May 5, 1866. Numerous towns claim to have had the first Memorial Day ceremony, but Waterloo, New York, earned the official honors as the place of origin.

"The Memorial Day Museum directly connects Waterloo's current history to the past. We show our guests how important Memorial Day was to us in 1865 and how we worked to be declared its birthplace in 1966. Our tour walks visitors from the 1866 efforts of Henry C. Wells and General John Murray to recognize those who fell in the war to 1966 when we presented evidence to Congress showing we were indeed the birthplace of Memorial Day. Many don't realize that our recognition

came from Congress and the president himself. Our museum illustrates the reverence with which Americans felt and continue to feel for those who gave their lives for our country. Some of the more impressive artifacts in our museum include our Civil War weapons and an original death certificate that was attached to a deceased soldier's coffin. Visitors are also impressed with the declaration naming Waterloo the birthplace of Memorial Day signed by President Lyndon Johnson and the pen that he used that day. The museum also recreates rooms indicative of life in Waterloo in 1866," says the executive director.

The Waterloo Library and Historical Society, with beginnings in 1875, oversees the Memorial Day Museum and the library, which opened in 1884, and the attached Terwilliger Hall, built in 1960.

The library, which is a Queen Anne Victorian–style building, and Terwilliger Hall sit behind the museum at 31 E. Williams St. Memorial Day artifacts were originally housed upstairs in the library before moving to their current location in 1966. Terwilliger Hall is open when the library is open and houses collections including authentic full-size vehicles, Native American artifacts, original maps, photographs, currency, antique guns, dolls, and the first pianos manufactured in Waterloo.

Women's Rights National Historical Park
136 Fall St., Seneca Falls; (315) 568-0024; nps.gov; open year-round; admission free

Women's Rights National Historical Park tells the story of the first women's rights convention, held in Seneca Falls, New York, on July 19–20, 1848. The park is composed of the visitor center, historic homes (open seasonally), and the Wesleyan Chapel.

The Wesleyan Chapel, built in 1843, was the location of the first Woman's Rights Convention (later called Seneca Falls Convention), where approximately three hundred people gathered to attend. On the morning of July 20, 1848, sixty-eight women signed the Declaration of Sentiments. The chief movers of the convention were Elizabeth Cady Stanton of Seneca Falls, Lucretia Mott of Philadelphia, Mary Ann McClintock and Jane Hunt of Waterloo, and Martha C. Wright of Auburn. It is considered by many historians to be the formal beginning of the women's rights movement in the United States. By the time the National Park Service purchased the church in 1985, there was very little of the original interior left, but after time a unique display of the original building emerged.

The Waterwall at Declaration Park is a one-hundred-foot-long bluestone water feature located between the visitor center and Wesleyan Chapel that is inscribed with the words of the Declaration of Sentiments.

Elizabeth Cady Stanton's House is just across the street from the park at 32 Washington St. Elizabeth Cady Stanton (1815–1902) was the main organizer of

the Seneca Falls Women's Rights Convention and primary author of the Declaration of Sentiments, and stirred strong emotions in audiences from the 1840s until her death in 1902. Stanton called her home the "Center of the Rebellion" or "Grassmere" during her family's fifteen years in Seneca Falls.

An interesting little factoid I found within a "Historical Sketch of Seneca Falls" article published in the July 7, 1887, *Seneca County Courier*, Seneca Falls, read: "A sequence to the Women's Rights movement was the 'Bloomer Costume' so-called because its adoption was advocated by Mrs. Amelia (Jenks) Bloomer (1818–1894), then resident of Seneca Falls, through her newspaper called The Lily. But Mrs. Bloomer did not originate the short dress, neither did she ever claim that it was her invention. It was first worn here by Mrs. Elizabeth Smith Miller, a daughter of Gerrit Smith, while on a visit to Mrs. Stanton. Mrs Stanton soon after adopted the costume, and was followed by Mrs. Bloomer and others."

The Corning Museum of Glass
1 Museum Way, Corning; (800) 732-6845 and (607) 937-5371; cmog.org; open year-round; admission charged

Absolutely everything and anything made of glass, from 3,500 years ago to the present, is in this rather large three-floor museum that ranks as one of the top sites to visit in NYS. All ages will enjoy this see-through museum.

"The Corning Museum of Glass offers a unique opportunity to experience glass from all angles. You can explore the history, art, and science of glass over the past thirty-five centuries. You can see the best in glass today in the Contemporary Art + Design galleries. You can watch hot glass come to life before your eyes at our daily live glassmaking demonstrations, and you can even try glassmaking for yourself during a Make Your Own Glass experience. The museum is dedicated to telling the story of a single, transformative material, and we strive to help our visitors see glass in a new light," says the manager of public relations.

With every turn you take there is something glistening in all shapes, colors, and sizes. The gallery areas are titled Frederick Carder (highlighting Steuben glass), Amphitheater Hot Shop, Contemporary Art & Design, Special Projects, West Bridge, 35 Centuries of Glass, Changing Exhibitions, Crystal City, Ben W. Heineman Sr. (a gallery of contemporary glass dated 1975 to 2000), and Innovation Focus and Gather. Throughout the day there are demonstrations taking place about every half hour titled Hot Glass, Glass Breaking, Optica; Fiber and Flameworking.

The Contemporary Art & Design gallery features areas on nature, body, design, history, and material. My favorite was the Nocturne 5, a black glass dress. In the Innovations area I liked the Pyrex cookware, the "Journey to the Moon—How Glass Got Us Here" exhibit, the Owens Bottle Machine, and items made with glass as flexible as silk. In a walk-through area I found a glass table, picture frame, and chair to be fascinating. Can you imagine sitting on a chair made of glass?

The areas in the 35 Centuries of Glass are titled Glass in Nature, Ancient Roman, Islamic World, Northern European, Venetian, 19th-Century European, Asian, American, Corning, New York: The Crystal City, Paperweights of the World, Tiffany Studios, and Modern. Some of my favorites in this gallery were a diorama of glassmakers around the world, figurines, etched goblets, trick drinking glasses, glass in religious observances, English beadwork, stained-glass windows, sulphides (made of glass-clay paste), rock-crystal glass, a Favrile "Pansy" vase, lightbulbs, a copy of the Liberty Bell, and a gold medal of the 1992 winter Olympics

Children might enjoy the scavenger hunt found on glassapp.cmog.org, stations where you place an object behind a water lens, and touch screens that tell a story.

They also have a cafe, extensive gift shop, make your own glass (additional fee) by reservation, and outdoor activities in the summer.

Bully Hill Vineyard Museum
8843 Greyton H. Taylor Memorial Dr., Hammondsport; (607) 868-3610; bullyhillvineyards.com; open Memorial Day to Columbus Day; admission free, donations appreciated

This museum, founded by the Taylor family, is a bit off the beaten path but well worth the trip, especially when you see the view overlooking Keuka Lake.

Greyton Hoyt Taylor (1903–1971) grew up in the family wine-making business started by his father Walter in 1880, and at the time of his death he was an officer of the Taylor Wine Company. Greyton listed his occupation as office manager in the

grape juice industry in the 1930 Hammondsport census, and in 1940 he was listed as a partner/manager of a wine cellar. Greyton and his son Walter S. (1931–2001) founded Bully Hill in 1970, and Walter established the museum in 1972. Walter designed and wrote his eye-catching wine labels and gave the wines names like Goat White, Fish Market White, Bulldog Baco Noir, Meat Market Red, Space Shuttle Rosé, and Thunder Road Blush.

"Greyton H. Taylor Wine Museum & Replica Cooper Shop is home to an extensive collection of antique winemaking equipment, Prohibition memorabilia (Prohibition years were 1920 to 1933), and historic artifacts from the early New York wine industry. There's even a collection of presidential wine glasses dating back to Abraham Lincoln! The Cooper Shop is a replica to some extent of the Hammondsport Cooperage Company (1875–1915). The building has an outstanding collection of cooper's tools, along with a seventy-minute film of the art of barrel-making. Memorabilia from the early days of the New York State wine industry may also be found," says the director of marketing.

The Walter S. Taylor Art Gallery is next to the museum and filled with over two hundred pieces of work from the brush of one of the most creative and provocative artists in the NYS wine industry. Many of the pieces on display can be recognized as wine labels. There are smaller collections of Walter's artwork in the tasting room and restaurant.

The winery offers walking tours of the estate and winemaking facility daily during the summer months (Memorial Day through Columbus Day), wine tasting, and a gift shop.

Waverly Museum
435 Chemung St., Waverly; (607) 240-8553; waverlymuseum.org; open year-round; admission free, donations appreciated

Everything about Waverly, founded in 1854 and the most populated village in Tioga County, which sits on the border with Pennsylvania, is in the Waverly Museum.

"The museum has over 1,300 framed historic photos displayed and dozens of large binders of additional photos and Waverly ephemera, bound newspapers, and history books on the area, as well as thousands of Waverly items dating back to the early 1800s. The JE Ranch Rodeo made Waverly the rodeo capital of the Northeast from about 1939 to 1956. Local restaurateur Ed O'Brien was instrumental in bringing the rodeo to the area. A large fire department display celebrates the long and proud history dating back to the 1850s. A local man, Elmer Bruffy, was a professional daredevil known as 'Daredevil Bruffy.' He toured the country doing dangerous stunts and feats of strength, and died during a performance of his hanging act," says a board member and curator.

Daredevil Bruffy's obituary, published in the September 26, 1945, *Binghamton Press*, Jasper, Alabama, read: "Daredevil Bruffy, billed as the 'man who hangs himself and lives,' tried it once too often last night at the Walker County Fair. Coroner Joe Legg said the performer, whose real name was Elmer L. Bruffy, placed a rope around his neck and leaped from a swing 120 feet above the ground. His fall was arrested after a 60-foot drop, but the apparatus in the loop of the rope around his neck failed. (Elmer was born 1894 in VA.)"

A preview of a JE Ranch Rodeo was published in the June 20, 1949, *Vestal News*, Waverly, New York: "Great preparations are being made on the JE Ranch here for the 11th Annual JE Ranch Rodeo which will take place July 1–4 and anticipating the biggest crowd that has ever attended the rodeo here. Col. Jim Eskew has doubled the seating capacity and has seats for well over 4,000 spectators. Fully a hundred cowboys and cowgirls are expected to gather here for this rodeo and among them will be many of national fame who have taken part in many of the biggest of the American rodeos."

Most of what you see in the museum was donated by Donald "Don" Merrill (1929–2019). He had his own business in Waverly, of course, Don Merrill Motors, which he operated for fifty years. The site of his business is where the museum currently sits. In his spare time he was a collector of everything, especially anything having to do with antique cars

The school area has lots of class pictures and full sets of yearbooks. On display in the Sugar Bowl, which was a favorite hangout from the 1950s to 1970s, is an original menu and table setting and lots of gum stuck under the table. There are countless photos of the trolley that operated until 1939. Besides the numerous photos of firemen from the four fire companies, in the fire department display there is a hood of a 1939 fire truck. Because it was such a big event, with a four-hour parade, there is an entire display on the 1910 Old Home Day. Daredevil Bruffy's display offers an assortment of his paraphernalia and photos. The National Protective Legion (NPL), a combination insurance company and lodge, has its own venue because the national headquarters was in Waverly. The O'Brien corner features a 1909 Studebaker buggy. The creamery gallery displays items from twenty-three creameries including samples of milk bottles. All the automobile dealers in town are represented with either pictures or advertisements. There are hundreds of items on display in the promotional area, from shoehorns to ice scrapers. The drug store area is an 1893 remodel of the Tracy, Olney, Clark Drug Store. In the theater section are playbills and even a movie seat from the Capital Theater. Two large feed mills are represented in the mill display. Bound newspapers, dating back to 1854, are stacked on shelves.

It is amazing that one man, Don Merrill, collected most of the museum's collection.

Tioga History Museum
110 Front St., Owego; (607) 687-2460; tiogahistory.org; open year-round; admission free, donations appreciated

The Tioga County Historical Society, founded in 1914, is committed to preserving the history of all the towns in Tioga County within its museum, research library, genealogical archive, and historic carriage house. The museum, which was erected under the bequest of Minnie Belle Wade (1867–1952) in 1959, sits in the Historical District of Owego, on the banks of the Susquehanna River.

Four roomy galleries, some permanent and some revolving, exist within the museum. I asked the executive assistant what his favorite artifact was and he immediately walked me over to a pristine Monarch Big 5 motorcycle. These rare, two-hundred-pound motorcycles were only made for a few years (1912–1915) by the Ives Motorcycle Corporation in Owego. Restoration of the motorcycle took place in 1973 and 1974 by a local group.

The president of the company was Willis Hubert Ives (1861–1932), who started out making bicycles, then was involved in the Empire Motor Cycle Company and the Reliance Motor Cycle Company, making motorcycles until about 1911. In 1917 Ives Manufacturing Company was making the Eureka Rim Compressor, a tool for removing and replacing automobile tires, for a company in Addison; in the 1920s they were making auto goods, then in the 1930s coat hangers.

An advertisement for the Monarch, published in the September 5, 1912, *Elmira Star-Gazette*, read: "The Monarch big 5 H.P. has made good and has proven the master of the highway. The best Motorcycle build for $200."

The Ives household in the 1900 Addison, Steuben County, New York census included Willis H. Ives, age thirty-nine; Alice Marie (Buckley), twenty-three (his second wife, married in January 1900); Gertrude, thirteen; Dwight, eight (children from his first marriage to Julia Newell in 1885); Ellen, sixty-three (his widowed mother). He listed his occupations as a manager/director of a bicycle factory. In the 1910 census, he is living in Owego with Alice (1875–1950) and son Theodore, and lists his occupation as manufacturer of motorcycles. Another son, Winston, is added to the Ives family in the 1915 Owego census, and his occupation is manufacturer of motors. Interesting artifacts I noticed were a Sporer, Carlson & Berry piano made in Owego, a beautiful carriage, an Ahwaga Ladder Co. #5 chandelier made in 1861 in New York City for $95, folk art portraiture oil paintings on every wall, Currier and Ives firefighter prints, a two-seater school desk, an 1840s map of Drake's Reservation in the village of Owego, and a very unique entranceway seat and umbrella holder. Most of the revolving displays are neat and orderly in glass cases.

The Tioga County Historical Society's vision statement is "Explore, Engage, Learn."

Museum of the Earth & Cayuga Nature Center— Paleontological Research Institution
1259 Trumansburg Rd., Ithaca; (607) 273-6623; museumoftheearth.org; open year-round; admission charged

The Museum of the Earth, opened in 2003 as part of the Paleontological Research Institution (PRI) and the Cayuga Nature Center, which partnered with PRI in 2013, are perfect for a family visit.

"The Museum of the Earth does a wonderful job integrating exhibits, videos, hands-on activities, fossils, and full-size dinosaur models to tell the story of the history of life and the Earth itself, including how the Upstate New York area was molded by the glaciers," says the manager of marketing.

Areas of focus are paleontology and earth science, evolution and biodiversity, conservation paleobiology, climate change and energy, and STEM education.

Extraordinary exhibits include the forty-four-foot Right Whale #2030 skeleton, which hangs above the Borg Warner Gallery; and the Hyde Park Mastodon, which is one of the most complete mastodon skeletons ever found, excavated by the Paleontological Research Institution staff.

Continue your journey from the past into the future with special exhibitions, lectures, and family-friendly programs such as Steggy the Stegosaurus in the

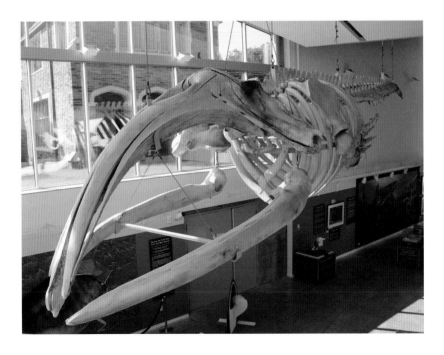

Jurassic-themed early learner Dino Zone, Devonian World, the "Dunkleosteus" (giant predatory fish) exhibit, the "Coelophysis" (a predatory dinosaur) exhibit, Quaternary World, the "Glacier" exhibit, and a giant heteromorph ammonite (more than four feet long). Journey 540 million years back in time through the five-hundred-foot mural titled Rock of Ages Sands of Time, then discover the diversity of life in the "Coral Reefs" exhibit and learn how changing climates shape the Earth.

While in the Dino Zone, children can dress as their favorite dinosaur, play inside a sauropod nest, learn all about the Jurassic world with books and hands-on activities, and watch Amelia the Quetzalcoatlus soaring above the Jurassic to Quaternary Theater.

There are also countless fossils (over seven million specimens) from all geological ages, skeletal reconstructions, and depictions of what the surrounding area looked like in the millennial past. You can even find and take home a trilobite or brachiopod fossil from the fossil lab.

The Cayuga Nature Center, which is five miles from the Museum of the Earth at 1420 Taughannock Blvd., offers miles of trails to hike, live animals in outdoor and indoor exhibits, TreeTops six-story tree house to climb, "Cayuga Lake: Past and Present" aquaria exhibit, a butterfly garden in the summer, and exhibits on the ecology of the Cayuga Basin.

The History Center in Tompkins County
110 N. Tioga St., Ithaca; (607) 273-8284; thehistorycenter.net; open year-round; admission free

The History Center highlights the history of Tompkins County and the Finger Lakes region through interactive displays focused on engaging with the public.

All museums have a history, and this one had quite a few moves. It had beginnings in the mid- and late 1800s that eventually led to the DeWitt Historical Society (named in honor of prominent Ithacan Simeon DeWitt) being re-formed in 1935. Artifacts were first housed in a room of a local bank, then were moved to the county courthouse the next year. In 1973 the museum moved to the Clinton House, then closed from 1992 to 1993 before reopening in the former Dean of Ithaca Building (now known as the Gateway). The new and current name came about in 2004. In May 2019 the History Center moved into the brand-new Tompkins Center for History & Culture.

"The great location of the History Center in Tompkins County on the Ithaca Commons, and the beautiful architecture and its rich history as a former bank and a former county clerk's office is my favorite aspect of the museum. Often the 'wow' factor is that many visitors don't know that we have a World War I-era airplane in

our gallery. Walking into a museum and seeing an airplane when it's not expected is a bit of a surprise," says the director of archives and research services.

Museumgoers first enter the exhibit hall via the Passage Through Time walkway, which begins with a Goyogoho:no' (Cayuga) creation myth and progresses through a timeline of Tompkins County history, from the famed building of the Clinton Hotel in 1828 to the election of Ithaca's first African American mayor, Svante Myrick, in 2011. The six PLACE (People, Land, Architecture, Culture, and Enterprise) Exhibit Towers each explore two local aspects of history and are changed twice a year. The main attraction in this area is the one-hundred-year-old Thomas Morse Aviation Scout S4-B, aka Tommy Plane, which was manufactured in Ithaca by the Thomas Morse Aviation Corporation in 1918. The last time it flew was in 2018. Take time to explore the Story Vault and listen to oral histories from local residents. Finally, there is a children's area that is a partial replica of the famed 1827 Eight Square Schoolhouse located in Dryden, New York. Children can explore how it would feel to be a student in Tompkins County over 150 years ago.

If interested in digging into local history or family genealogy, the Cornell Local Research Library and Thaler/Howell Archives overlooks the exhibit hall.

Hoffman Clock Museum
121 High St., Newark; (585) 586-2942; hoffmanclockmuseum.org; open year-round; admission free

Step into a "time machine" and learn about the history of timekeeping in the Hoffman Clock Museum, housed in the Newark Public Library. Its unique collection of timepieces from around the world has something for everyone and includes over three hundred clocks, watches, and tools, with an emphasis on the history of NYS clockmakers.

The NYS collection honors clockmakers such as Abner Jones, Henry Loomis, Jared Arnold, Lawyer Byington, Asa Munger, and many more. Some of the NYS clocks on display include Ithaca calendar clocks, a Juvet globe clock circa 1883, a Samuel Chubbock tall case clock, an Empire shelf clock circa 1835, and a Monitor shelf clock.

Many of the timepieces on display are from Augustus L. Hoffman's (1856–1945) collection. Hoffman promoted the formation of the clock museum, which opened in 1954. He was a retail jeweler and a watchmaker who owned a jewelry shop in Newark for thirty years.

"Some visitors like the Timby Solar clock, circa 1863, which in addition to being a clock has a rotating terrestrial globe; or the Aaron Crane Torsion Pendulum clock, which operates for an entire year on a single winding and was invented by one of America's horological geniuses. Younger visitors often like the cuckoo clock or the IBM time clock where they can punch a time card," says the assistant curator.

A horologist is someone who studies the measurement of time.

Visitors also like the Black Forest organ/flute clock, which was made in Furt-wangen, Germany. The organ consists of forty-six pipes in two ranks (groups). The music is recorded on a wooden barrel/cylinder that is five inches in diameter and fifteen inches long. It plays eight different German folk tunes, each lasting about forty seconds. Across the top of the case are six wooden musicians, which raise their instruments and move as the music plays. The musical part of the clock is attributed to C. Muckle and the shield/face is signed by Leodegar Dufner.

The curators' favorite clocks reflect Yankee ingenuity, which fostered horological innovation that transferred to other American industries in the early 1800s. America's most important clockmaker, Eli Terry, revolutionized manufacturing processes by simplifying the movement, construction methods, and production means to reduce manufacturing time and costs. The museum has several Terry clocks including a wooden-works Porter Contract tall clock, of which fewer than fifteen examples are known. Other horological innovations include a Joseph Ives clock powered by a wagon spring, and a Herman and Clark clock regarded as the first American clock powered by coiled springs.

Digital clocks and watches are nice, but to me these timepieces are way more interesting.

Hotchkiss Peppermint Museum
95 Water St., Lyons; (315) 946-4596; lyonsheritagesociety.org; open July and Aug or by appointment; admission free

Situated on the banks of the original "Clinton's Ditch"/Erie Canal near Lock 27 sits the office, now museum, of H. G. Hotchkiss, the "Peppermint Oil King." This one-of-a-kind museum tells the story of the international peppermint oil industry and its influence on the economic growth of Lyons, Wayne County, and western New York.

Hiram Gilbert Hotchkiss (1810–1897) established the H.G. Hotchkiss Essential Oil Company with his brother Leman in 1839. Prior to Hotchkiss's rise to Peppermint King, the European markets were king, until Europe wanted Wayne County peppermint oil. Hiram and his wife, Mary Ashley (1813–1884), had eleven children, which enabled the company to be operated by Hotchkiss heirs until 1982. Anne Hotchkiss, who operated the company for forty-five years, was the last of the family but had no heirs, so she sold it to a company from Indiana. The new company continued operations in Lyons until 1990, and then the Lyons Heritage Society bought the H. G. Hotchkiss office, which was built in 1884. It is one of three industries on the canal system left intact.

During its heyday the international prize-winning (seventeen gold medals) peppermint could be smelled for miles along the Erie Canal, because just about every farmer in or near Lyons was growing peppermint as a cash crop. The peppermint plants were distilled into oil, which was bottled in twenty-one-ounce blue bottles (later in amber bottles) made in nearby Clyde, New York. Peppermint oil is mostly used for confections/candy, but it is also used in dentifrices, ointments, cold remedies, gum, and pharmaceutical products.

When Hiram died in 1897, his company was called H.G. Hotchkiss International Prize Medal Essential Oil Company and was worth several million dollars. Hotchkiss had created a new name for the town of Lyons, the "Peppermint Capital of the World."

Permanent exhibits that are on two floors and the basement include H. G. Hotchkiss's office, the bottling room, chemical lab, filter room, and fanning mill, tools, and a Lyons history room with artifacts and art from Lyons's history. The director told me about some interesting artifacts such as a Bavarian cut glass "show globe" used in a World Fair to display the oil, an 1873 safe and 1865 desk, original 1840s bottles and crates, an original bookkeeper's desk, the cornerstone of a larger factory that was built in 1862 and now gone, an 1812 wooden basement door with canawlers' (folks who had occupations pertaining to the canal) graffiti, original certificates of gold medal awards (two of which were signed by Prince Albert and Napoleon III), and a vault in the basement that was intended to protect the peppermint oil from fires.

During my research I found two other "Peppermint Kings" in Michigan, but H. G. Hotchkiss came first.

Dundee Area Historical Society
26 Seneca St., Dundee; (607) 243-7047; dundeeareahistory.com; open May through Oct

The Dundee Area Historical Society offers two sites to visit, the Hoyt Coal Weigh Station and the Old Schoolhouse Museum.

The Old Schoolhouse was built in 1891 using bricks from the 1861 schoolhouse and was in use until 1938. It fell into disrepair, then was rescued by the Society in 1972 and opened to the public in 1975.

The main floor has a parlor setup, and upstairs has two exhibit areas and a research library. One room has a military theme and is full of artifacts, uniforms from the Civil War through the Korean War, and displays about Freemasons, IOOF (Independent Order of Odd Fellows), and Legion regalia. Another room is devoted to the Starkey Seminary and assorted one-room schoolhouses in Yates County.

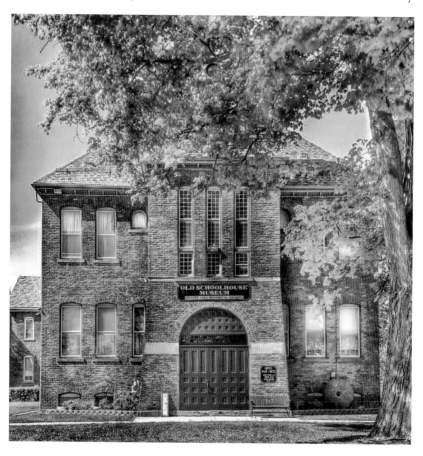

Exhibits in this room pertain to children from cradle to graduation and includes toys and dolls from around the world.

Eddytown was the home of the original Starkey Seminary, which opened in 1842. The school then relocated a mile down the road in about 1900, became known as the Palmer Institute-Starkey Seminary in 1902, closed its doors in 1936, reopened as Lakemont Academy for Boys from 1939 to 1970, became Glen Springs Academy from 1972 to 1974, and later opened as Freedom Village USA.

An advertisement published in the July 27, 1912, *Evening Post*, New York City, described the Palmer Institute-Starkey Seminary as a "[b]eautiful site on Seneca Lake. Boarding school for both sexes of 14 years and upward. Regents standards. Splendid training for best colleges and business. Advanced courses for young women in art and music. Special attention to health. Secure rooms early, for fall entrance. Rates $250 to $275. Martyn Summerbell PH.D."

The Hoyt Coal Weigh Station is just behind the Old Schoolhouse Museum and houses various farm implements, examples of Dundee businesses, and the old scale used to weigh coal. There are also exhibits on the berry and dairy industries of Yates County.

Yates County History Center
107 Chapel St., Penn Yan; (315) 536-7318; yatespast.org;
open year-round; admission free, suggested donation

The Yates County History Center (YCHC) encompasses three buildings: the Oliver House Museum, L. Caroline Underwood Museum, and Scherer Carriage House Museum. The YCHC is one of the oldest in NYS, and has been actively collecting, preserving, and interpreting Yates County history since 1860.

The eighteen-room, Italianate-style Oliver House Museum was built in 1852 by Dr. Andrew Oliver as a wedding gift for his son William. Miss Carrie Oliver (1868–1942) was the last Oliver to live in the house. Carrie left the house and its contents to the Village of Penn Yan for perpetual use as a museum. The Oliver House features six Victorian period rooms furnished with an eclectic mix of the Olivers' belongings and the collections of the historical society. There is also a Native American exhibit as well as changing local history exhibits.

The Underwood Museum houses Miss Underwood's collections, with two rooms of permanent displays, and the Gracey Gallery, with changing exhibits. Miss Lucy Caroline Underwood (1902–1998) was known as a well-loved teacher, an avid collector, and a passionate supporter of local history. A partial list of some of the artifacts on display are a rosewood parlor set, an eight-day clock, a pair of Chinese vases, eleven Hitchcock chairs, and a blue coverlet with the corner block "Caroline Cadmus, Benton, NY 1835." The Spencer Research Center, which contains genealogical information pertaining to Yates County, and the Frank Swann Archives are also housed in the Underwood Museum.

The Scherer Carriage House, behind the Underwood Museum, is the permanent home of the YCHC's premier exhibit, "Jemima Wilkinson: The Publick Universal Friend." Jemima, who was brought up in the Quaker religion, was said to have been near death during an illness in 1776. When she recovered, she claimed to have received a revelation from God and considered herself as non-gender, rebuked her given name, and would only respond to Publick Universal Friend or Friend. "My favorite exhibit, and the one that wows people the most, is our exhibit about the Public Universal Friend, Jemima Wilkinson. She was the first American woman to start her own religion—a brave pioneer and preacher. She brought about three hundred followers here to settle the wilderness now known as Yates County," says the administrative assistant.

The exhibit about Publick Universal Friend Jemima Wilkinson (1752–1819) includes the Friend's portrait, Bible, hat, saddle, and coachee (carriage). The Society of Universal Friends had a couple more leaders following Friend's death, but the group died out by the 1860s.

The Scherer Carriage House was named for Mrs. Doris (Coates) Scherer, a generous benefactor of Yates County History Center. All three museums are within walking distance of one another.

FASNY Museum of Firefighting
117 Harry Howard Ave., Hudson; (518) 822-1875;
fasnyfiremuseum.com; open year-round; admission charged

Absolutely, positively everything pertaining to three centuries of firefighting in NYS with numerous hands-on activities for all ages and over sixty fire engines. There's even have a museum dog, a dalmatian named Molly, so named for one of the first female firefighters, Molly Williams.

It takes a few roads to get here, but the short journey from the main road is easy and well marked with signs for the museum. The museum sits within a complex of buildings and is next to the FASNY Fireman's Home for volunteer firemen and a fireman's cemetery.

Upon entering the museum there are oodles of fire trucks on the floor, fire department banners from all over NYS hanging from the ceiling, and fire department patches from around the world on the walls. There are pumper, tanker, and ladder trucks, but my favorite, on the first floor, was a 1970 "C" class racing car, "Blue Jays," from Sayville, New York. There is also an interesting display of hundreds of gallon-size water bottles on the wall, with names of museum supporters on them, which gives a visual for the amount of water it takes to fill a fire truck.

The second floor houses older fire apparatus, more banners, and exhibit areas titled Mattydale Hall (with rotating exhibits), Volunteer Hall, and Steamer Hall. "Then, Now & Always: Fire Fighting from the Cradle of Ancient Rome through the 1900s" is in Volunteer Hall and offers display cases that trace the evolution of firefighting starting with the 22 BC Roman Empire. Artifacts displayed that I thought were quite unique included 1600s wooden rattles that were used to alert townspeople of fires; 1700s leather water buckets, a flambeau torch used to light the way at night, and a bed key used to quickly disassemble a bed and save it from a fire; 1800s fire marks (metal plaques attached to the house) that denoted how much insurance coverage was on a house and a smoke helmet made by Siebe, Gorman & Co. that pumped air into the helmet; and 1900s flashlights, fire extinguishers, 1970s SCBAs (self-contained breathing apparatus), and a 1975 Motorola Minitor pager for letting firemen know there was a fire to go to.

The oldest piece of fire apparatus is the 1731 Newsham engine, named Hayseeds, from New York City. As the story goes, two fire engines, built by Richard Newsham in England, arrived in New York City in December 1731 aboard the ship Beaver. The same story pertains to the Deluge #1 fire engine that sits in the Old

Stone Fort Museum in Schoharie, New York. So it appears that the two oldest fire engines are still in NYS only fifty miles apart.

In the Steamer Hall is the "Social Favor & Local Flavor: The Firehouse of the 1800s" exhibit. My favorite in this area was the Black Ball Box used for voting on new members; a white ball was a yes vote and black was a no. Another exhibit featured in Steamer Hall is "Legacy: Robert Fulton and the Commercial Advent of the Steam Engine." Here you will find the 1855 John Rodgers Hand Pumper, also known as "The Sun" or "Big Sun," which was used during the Civil War in Virginia, then went to New York City. A couple of my other favorites were Continental Bucket Co. No. 1 from Jamaica, New York; a wagon full of water-filled leather buckets; a Clapp & Jones steam engine made in Hudson; and a memorial to the 343 firefighters who lost their lives at the World Trade Center in New York City on September 11, 2001.

Displays have thorough descriptions, and staff members are stationed throughout the museum so that you can always get answers to your questions.

Olana State Historic Site
5720 State Rte. 9G, Hudson; (518) 828-1872; olana.org; open year-round; admission charged

Step back into the 1890s by visiting the Persian-inspired mansion that was the home to Frederic Edwin Church, one of the major figures in the Hudson River School of landscape painting, and the estate he called Olana.

Frederic Edwin Church (1826–1900) married Isabel Mortimer Carnes (1836–1899) in 1860. They had two children that died young, then had four more children who lived to adulthood: Frederic, Theodore, Louis, and Isabel. They started building the house on "the Farm," which later became known as Olana, the year Louis was born in 1870. The mansion was completed in 1872, but Church often revised or altered the house until about 1891.

Church showed artistic talent early on, so his parents sent him to Catskill, New York, to study with landscape painter Thomas Cole from 1844 to 1846. His connection with Cole brought him into the fold of the Hudson River School, which was not an actual classroom but a group of painters who hung out together because they worked in a similar style. Church's The Catskill Creek, painted in 1845, is a perfect example of the Hudson River School style and hangs in the mansion.

Church moved to New York City following his time with Cole. He traveled quite a bit, sometimes with family and sometimes with other artists, around the United States and the world, so his landscape paintings depict sights from numerous areas. Church and his family considered Olana their home, but they also kept a connection to NYC through the years.

Some of the items you might see in the mansion are dozens of carpets from all regions of the Middle East; two tile fireplaces by Ali Mohammed Isfahani, a nineteenth-century Persian ceramist, purchased through a shop in New York City; the family's household china; a sculpture by Erastus Dow Palmer titled Sleep, circa 1858; Lockwood de Forest desk circa 1882–1890 carved in his workshop in Ahmedabad, India; David Vinckboons' Tobias and the Angel, 1619, oil on canvas; Frederic Edwin Church's El Khasné, Petra, 1874 oil on canvas; and a collection of sombreros and Mexican folk art.

"Olana is a three-dimensional work of art created over forty years by America's greatest landscape artist. What fascinates visitors most is the experience of moving through the 250-acre historical landscape that culminates in the great house and the feeling that you have seen it through Church's eyes. People are very surprised to learn that Church designed all aspects of Olana—its landscape, its carriage roads, and its architecture," says the president of The Olana Partnership.

"Our visitors love the views and vistas at Olana. Frederic Church designed Olana as an observatory where we can experience the remarkable views of the Hudson River, the mountains, the ever-changing weather patterns, and the expansive sky. The unique home that he built for his family is a treasure house filled with art and collections acquired from all over the world. Together, the house and landscape create an immersive environment designed to surprise and delight our visitors. Our guided tours help visitors understand Church's life and work. The vast landscape provides a place of quiet reflection that is free and open to all," says the director.

Locust Grove Estate
2683 South Rd., Poughkeepsie; (845) 454-4500, lgny.org;
open Apr through Dec for guided tours only; admission charged

Locust Grove, which overlooks the Hudson River, has something for everyone: a historic Italianate-style mansion built in 1851, a visitor center with art galleries, five miles of hiking trails, and restored gardens that feature dozens of heirloom varieties of flowers and vegetables that you will not see anywhere else.

The mansion was a summer home designed for artist and inventor Samuel Finley Breese Morse (1791–1872) by architect Alexander Jackson Davis. Morse was a portrait painter and contributed to the inventions of a single-wire telegraph and Morse code. He had two wives and seven children, the first being born in 1819 and the last in 1857. After Samuel's death in 1872, the family did not spend much time in their summer villa and eventually rented it to William Hopkins and Martha (Innis) Young, a wealthy couple from Poughkeepsie.

The Youngs furnished the house with family heirlooms and bought it in 1901. In the 1900 Poughkeepsie census, William is a forty-five-year-old lawyer, Martha is forty-three, Annette is fifteen, Innis is twelve, and there are two servants. They added a larger dining room wing, guest bedrooms, central heat, hot and cold running water, and electric lighting so that their daughter Annette and son Innis could live there year-round. When Annette's brother Innis died in 1953, she became the sole owner of Locust Grove Estate and other family holdings. When Annette died in 1975, she left a legacy that established a not-for-profit foundation to maintain Locust Grove as a museum and nature preserve. The estate opened to the public in 1979 and today features the Young family's fifteen-thousand-piece collection of furniture, a collection of Hudson River School paintings, and decorative arts just as they were used in the early years of the twentieth century.

In the gardens and grounds Morse found natural features that he used to frame views, create vistas, and provide comfortable settings in which to relax and enjoy the beauty of the landscape. The Youngs built scenic carriage drives and expanded the formal gardens. Today the Cutting Garden preserves Martha Young's unique style and plant collection.

"The Locust Grove gardens include a collection of more than seven hundred heirloom peonies planted in the 1890s (more than a century ago!), which are still blooming today," says the director.

Two hundred years ago the kitchen garden provided fresh produce for the residents of the estate. Today the restored kitchen garden provides a place for visitors to learn about the wide variety of vegetables and fruits grown centuries ago. The Samuel Morse Museum Pavilion is home to an exhibit that honors the two careers, artist and inventor, that Morse was successful at. Included in the exhibit are original paintings, drawings, and sculptures from all phases of his career. In the Telegraph Gallery, there are reproductions of Morse's early electromagnetic telegraph models.

The Transverse Gallery in Locust Grove's Visitor Welcome Center hosts four to six solo exhibits by contemporary artists each year.

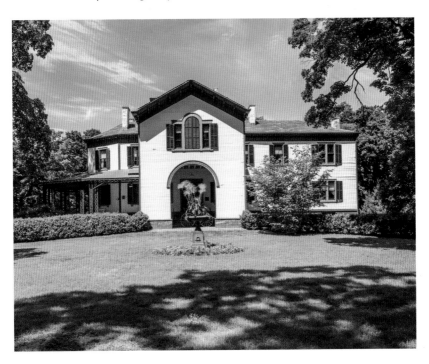

Vanderbilt Mansion
**81 Vanderbilt Park Rd., Hyde Park; (845) 229-7770;
nps.gov/vama/index.htm; open year-round for guided tours;
admission charged**

This fifty-four-room mansion of Beaux-Arts architectural style (taught at the Ecole des Beaux-Arts school in Paris), which overlooks the Hudson River, was constructed between 1896 and 1899 for Frederick William and Louise Holmes (Anthony) Vanderbilt. The 211-acre Vanderbilt estate is a perfect example of a Gilded Age country palace, illustrating the political, economic, social, cultural, and demographic changes that occurred as America industrialized in the years after the Civil War.

"The earliest development of lands that became the Vanderbilts' Hyde Park began in 1764 when Dr. John Bard purchased land on the east side of the Albany Post Road. Dr. Bard built Red House and developed the agricultural aspects of the eastern section of the property that continued through Frederick Vanderbilt's occupancy. The Bard family owned the property until 1821," says the acting chief of interpretation.

Dr. John Bard had called his estate "Hyde Park" in honor of Edward Hyde, who was Lord Cornbury and governor of New York. In 1804, a tavern keeper whose business was slow named his tavern "Hyde Park Inn," much to the annoyance of Dr. Bard. Miller, the tavern keeper, applied for a post office to be located at his inn, which was nothing unusual for those times. The request was granted as the "Hyde Park Post Office." This officially changed the settlement's name from Stoutenburgh to Hyde Park in 1812.

Public rooms in the mansion on the ground floor are the central Elliptical Hall, a dining room, and a living room; off the Elliptical Hall are the lobby, den, Gold Room, Grand Stair Hall, and lavatory. The second-floor rooms are Mrs. Vanderbilt's suite of bedroom, boudoir, and bathroom; Mr. Vanderbilt's bedroom and bathroom, guest bedrooms and baths; and the linen room. The third floor contains five additional guest bedrooms and a servants' hall separated from the guests' rooms by a door at the main staircase. The Vanderbilt estate had electric lighting before the surrounding area, powered by a hydroelectric plant built on the estate on the Crumb Elbow stream.

A few of the mansion's unique artifacts include planetaria, or orreries, mechanical models of the solar system, which were purchased from Heilbronner and made by George Adams the Elder 1708–1773, Fleet Street, London; and a Steinway piano with a gilded and decorated case, originally made for Frederick Vanderbilt's 693 Fifth Avenue house and sold to him on October 23, 1880. The piano, as recorded in the Steinway ledgers, was finished in rosewood and one of one hundred completed in 1880. It was later decorated by Martine and was "one of the rarest and costliest in the city." The piano was brought to Hyde Park at some time after the home was

constructed. Hanging in the living room and vestibule are "The History of Troy" Tapestries, which are four tapestries illustrating the history of Troy that were made in the seventeenth century in the workshop of Martin Reynbouts. In Greek mythology, the Trojan War was waged against the city of Troy by the Achaeans after Paris of Troy took Helen from her husband, Menelaus, the king of Sparta. Each tapestry in the set illustrates an important event in the story.

I visited this site years ago and still vividly remember the opulence of the mansion.

Museum Village at Old Smith's Clove
1010 Rte. 17M, Monroe; (845) 782-8248; museumvillage.org; open Apr through Nov; admission charged

Museums usually come about and operate due to a committee of history lovers, but not Museum Village. This unique open-air museum, situated in the Hudson Valley, was organized, furnished, and then opened in July 1950 by Roscoe William Smith. All age groups will find something of interest in this collection of nineteenth-century rural Americana. You might make a dipped candle, watch the blacksmith, or take a selfie next to Harry the Mastodon.

The ancestors of founder Roscoe Smith (1877–1976) were among the early settlers of Monroe, New York. Roscoe was, for the most part, a self-educated entrepreneur who started forming small enterprises as a teenager, then hit on his life's work in 1905. He founded the Orange and Rockland Electric Company that became Rockland and Orange Utilities, which he retired from in 1970. These companies would afford him the ability to create Museum Village.

Roscoe started collecting artifacts that helped America grow, mostly craft tools and mechanical devices, about the year 1920. He had a vision of educating future generations about these soon-to-be-gone implements. Along the way to founding and then operating his museum he had help from his sisters Mrs. Meta S. Bush and Mrs. Edna S. Seaman; his wife, Mrs. Ina (Allen) Smith; and son Leland A. and daughter Margaret Elizabeth (Mrs. Richmond Frederick Meyer). In 1961, Smith surrendered his ownership of the museum to the New York State Board of Regents.

"Museum Village is a unique and inviting open-air historical museum that offers visitors the opportunity to explore vignettes of nineteenth-century American life. Using a large collection of eclectic artifacts, the museum provides hands-on educational experiences and exhibits that illustrate the transition from a rural to an industrial culture and economy in America. Visitors to the museum are often surprised by how many items are in our vast collection of eclectic artifacts. From our original eighteenth-century log cabin to our extensive nineteenth-century textile collection, to our Corliss steam engine, and everything in between—there is something of interest for everyone here at Museum Village," says the director of marketing.

You can tour Museum Village at your own pace, or if you like, guided tours are available in the summer. Many of the buildings have costumed interpreters that are prepared to demonstrate nineteenth-century living. Self-guided tours are especially nice for families with younger children because you have the ability to spend as much or as little time as you want in the twenty buildings that surround the village green.

The structures that surround Smith's village green were either built on-site or moved from other locations. As you stroll around the green, or square, as some call it, you will be able to visit the buildings that made up a village from more than one hundred years ago, including a barn, blacksmith shop, broom shop, candle shop, energy building, farm tools, firehouse, livery, log cabin, natural history building, pottery shop, playhouse, print shop, salt box house, stone schoolhouse, wagon shop, weave shop, the Vernon drug store and Merritt store, and a changing exhibits building.

A highlight of your visit could be Harry the Mastodon, which is housed in the natural history building. Harry, who is about twelve thousand years old and stands eleven feet high and twenty-three feet long, is one of only three complete specimens of a mastodon in the world. The mastodon was a local resident that was excavated in 1947 in Harriman, New York, next door to Monroe.

Special events are offered during the year such as plays in the playhouse; lectures; Mineral, Jewelry, Gem & Fossil Show; a Civil War reenactment; Hudson Valley Fiesta Latina; No-Scare Halloween; Thanksgiving Tasting & Toy Drive; and Christmas at The Village.

I visited here in the mid-1960s, and it sparked my interest in American history. As a kid I had always wondered how they came up with the name Smith's Clove. Now, following my research Smith is easy to figure out and Clove is an old word for valley or cleft.

Museum Village also has a visitor center, gift shop, and snack bar. Visitors are welcome to bring their own picnic lunch and eat at the picnic tables by the snack bar.

Washington's Headquarters State Historic Site
84 Liberty St., Newburgh; (845) 562-1195; parks.ny.gov/historic-sites; open year-round for guided tours; admission charged

This is the first publicly owned historic site in the nation, which opened to the public in 1850. General George Washington, commander-in-chief of the Continental Army, utilized numerous homes as headquarters during the Revolution, in New York, New Jersey, Connecticut, Massachusetts, Pennsylvania, Delaware, Maryland, and Rhode Island, but he spent the most time in Newburgh at what is also known as the Hasbrouck House.

The Revolution, also known as America's War of Independence, took place from 1775 to 1783, and George Washington (1732–1799) was the first president of our new country, from 1789 to 1797. George Washington, his wife Martha, and their staff headquartered and resided in Jonathan and Tryntje (Dubois) Hasbrouck's fieldstone farmhouse for sixteen and a half months from April 1782 to August 1783. The Hasbrouck House, which overlooks the Hudson River, was built in 1750 and is the oldest or one of the oldest houses in the city of Newburgh. It was here that Washington made some of his most important contributions to shaping the American republic: He rejected the suggestion of an American monarchy; ended the Newburgh Conspiracy, thus preventing potential military control of the government; created the Badge of Military Merit, forerunner of the Purple Heart; circulated an influential letter to state governors outlining the key principles he felt necessary for the new republic; and announced the cessation of hostilities, which ended the fighting of the Revolutionary War.

"Hasbrouck House is furnished to reflect Washington's stay, and it is a unique experience to walk within the rooms of Hasbrouck House, interpreted as if General Washington was in residence. The immersive experience is like no other! Over 1,300 artifacts are on view in the museum, including some unique objects: the only known salvaged section of the original Revolutionary War boom and chain that spanned the Hudson to block British ships from coming upriver from New York City, and a lock of George Washington's hair, which is a fan favorite," says the site manager.

After visiting the Hasbrouck House and museum, walk over to the Tower of Victory, also on the seven-acre site, completed in about 1890 to commemorate the centennial of Washington's stay, and climb the steps to the newly restored belvedere to enjoy the scenic view (weather permitting).

I have fond memories of visiting this site to this day, even though I visited as a kid a gazillion years ago. I remember being enthralled by walking in a house that Washington slept in.

Boscobel House and Gardens
1601 Rte. 9D, Garrison; (845) 265-3638; boscobel.org; open May through Oct; admission charged

Boscobel House, of Federal-style architecture, was built between 1804 and 1808 in Montrose, New York, but that is not where some of it is now. What an amazing life this house, now surrounded by lush gardens and overlooking the Hudson River, has had.

The house was built by States Morris (1755–1806) and Elizabeth Corne (Kennedy) Dyckman (1776–1823), but States had only witnessed the foundation of his dream mansion when he died. The idea of the house came to States while he was on business in England from 1800 to 1803. States saw and liked the Boscobel estate in Shropshire and decided to use the same name for his home. Elizabeth carried on the building project, and when finished she furnished it in a style associated with the decorative accessories that States had sent her from England five years before. Elizabeth moved into the residence with their only surviving child, Peter Corne Dyckman (1797–1824) and was the overseer of the household and the 250-acre farm. Following Elizabeth and Peter's deaths, the home was lived in by Peter's wife,

Susan, whom he had married in 1819, and daughter Eliza. Dyckman heirs occupied the home until 1888, then assorted owners lived in Boscobel until 1923 when the Westchester County Parks Commission purchased the land to create Crugers Park. The house remained vacant until a group of people formed Boscobel Inc. in 1942 to preserve and maintain the house. In 1945 the Veterans Administration purchased the property and made good use of it, but still ignored the house. Ten years later a contractor won the bid to demolish the house for $35. Boscobel Restoration Inc. raised enough funds to stop the demolition partway through the job, acquired portions of the structure, carted the pieces fifteen miles away to Garrison, and started putting it back together in 1957. Boscobel was opened to the public in 1961.

Rooms in the house include an entrance hall, drawing room, rear drawing room, dining room, library, Elizabeth Dyckman's bedroom, a guest room, Peter Dyckman's bedroom, and a skullery (small kitchen).

"Everywhere you look at Boscobel there are references to beautiful landscapes—the views framed by the panoramic windows, and the landscapes that adorn furniture, ceramics, paintings, prints, even humble storage boxes. Natural light animates Boscobel's architecture and richly figured mahogany, glazed ceramics, cut glass, and textured upholstery, changing with the times of day and seasons, and responding to the movement of every visitor that passes through. My favorites are always changing, but certainly include the Gibson & Davis piano, the Marks girandoles (ornamental candlesticks), the Phyfe dressing table, the Albany-made mirror in the dining room, and the eagle-topped mirrors in the library—the mirrored surfaces literally enable modern-day visitors to see themselves reflected in Hudson Valley design, history, and nature. Boscobel's sixty-eight public acres overlook the very section of the Hudson River that George Washington considered the key to winning the American Revolution," says the executive director/curator.

Putnam History Museum
63 Chestnut St., Cold Spring; (845) 265-4010; putnamhistorymuseum.org; open year-round; admission free, donations suggested

This museum has two dedicated galleries displaying artifacts and information related to the history and heritage of Putnam County and a permanent "West Point Foundry" exhibition that traces the history of the foundry's manufacture of iron products.

The West Point Foundry was established in 1818 by Gouverneur Kemble (1786–1875) and closed in 1911. The foundry got its name because it sat across the Hudson River from the US military academy West Point, which had been established in 1802. Kemble's company manufactured iron products and became one of

the major industrial sites in the United States, especially during the Civil War, when it produced the Parrott cannon designed by Robert Parker Parrott in 1860. Included in the "Foundry" exhibition are photographs, artifacts, paintings, maps, videos, and a fully restored ten-pounder Parrott Rifle. The Parrott, which weighs 150 pounds, is a cast-iron muzzle-loading rifle cannon.

Robert Parker Parrott (1804–1877) graduated from West Point in 1824 and became the superintendent of the foundry in 1836. He purchased the foundry from Gouverneur Kemble a few years later and also married Mary, a sister of Kemble's, soon after. Artillery was often tested by shooting across the Hudson River at the mountains; in the 1990s some of the ammunition was discovered unexploded. Parrott resigned from the management of the foundry in 1867 but continued to experiment with artillery designs until his death.

The foundry also built one of the first successful American-made locomotives in 1830; manufactured the USS *Spencer*, a revenue cutter that was the first American-made iron ship built in 1843; and had a part in the making of the steam frigate Merrimack in 1855.

"Tourists are most often surprised by the West Point Foundry's significant role in the American Civil War. They are also surprised to learn that Cold Spring, New York, was one of the first company towns in the United States," says the director.

The Putnam History Museum also offers a lecture series and a Special Collections Library with an amazingly diverse collection to share with the public in the library and through exhibitions.

One of the West Point Foundry buildings, the central office, is off-site in the West Point Foundry Preserve.

Haverstraw Brick Museum
12 Main St., Haverstraw; (845) 947-3505; haverstrawbrickmuseum.org; open year-round; admission free

This museum is dedicated to preserving the cultural and historical past of the Village of Haverstraw and the vibrant brick industry that created it.

Haverstraw, first named Warren until 1874, is situated on the Hudson River. Huge deposits of yellow and blue clay along the Hudson River shoreline created the brick industry, and the same waterway made for a convenient and necessary mode of transportation for delivering the bricks to New York City and beyond. The first brick factory was established by a Dutch settler, Jacob VanDyke, in 1771, who made bricks manually and used ovens to temper the clay. In 1815 an Englishman, John Wood, improved the brick-making process by using a vented wooden mold, which led to a boom in the industry that continued into the 1940s.

Interesting insight into the brick industry was published in the August 11, 1885, Albany (NY) Argus: "'Down the River.' At the present time fifty firms are engaged in the manufacture of brick at Haverstraw, giving employment to nearly 3,000 men, employing 170 machines, and turning out in one year 302,617,000 brick, which would build a wall ten feet high and one foot thick 220 miles long."

"Our museum chronicles the history of the earliest settlers in the United States continuously from 1616 to the present through the lens of the brick manufacturing industry, the factory owners' families, and their descendants. Through collections of private historical papers, photographs, and oral histories from the families' descendants, the museum tells a unique story of immigration, integration, and manufacturing innovation from the 1700s to the 1940s. Tourists are often surprised by how far back in American history our story goes and how important the brick-making industry was to the building of New York and other cities in the United States," says the museum staff.

Some of the significant buildings built with Haverstraw bricks include the original Yankee Stadium 1928–2008 (Goldbrick Co., Rose Brick Yard), Empire State Building (Rose Brickyard), New York Stock Exchange (Rose Brickyard), Singer Tower (Rose Brickyard), Waldorf Astoria (Rose Brickyard), Seventh Regiment Armory, 34th Street Chelsea Market, and Museum of Natural History.

Trailside Museums & Zoo
3020 Seven Lakes Dr., Bear Mountain; (845) 786-2701, ext. 265; trailsidezoo.org; open year-round; admission charged

Trailside Museums & Zoo sits within Bear Mountain State Park on the west bank of the Hudson River. Four different museums are situated along a self-guided trail: Herpetology House and the Nature Study, Geology, and History Museums. Some of the trail is part of the Appalachian Trail.

The Herpetology House, or perhaps more easily known as the "Amphibians, Reptiles, and Fish Museum" houses a variety of local snakes, lizards, turtles, frogs, salamanders, and fish.

The Nature Study Museum offers a learning experience on local wildlife. The mounted specimens give the visitor a close-up look at birds and bird eggs, small mammals, and dragonflies, butterflies, and other insects. Plus there are some animal skulls.

Discover the region's geology and animals of ancient times, including a mastodon skull, in the Geology Museum. Learn that extractive industry started in the colonial era with the mining of magnetite iron ore, which was processed in nearby furnaces.

Delve into the layers of history at signs along the trail and Fort Clinton and exhibits inside the History Museum.

Assorted programs and nature walks are offered throughout the year.

Horace Greeley House
100 King St., Chappaqua; (914) 238-4666; newcastlehs.org; open year-round; admission by donation

Horace Greeley House was built between 1852 and 1854 as part of the development of downtown Chappaqua, a hamlet of New Castle, after the arrival of the railroad.

Horace Greeley (1811–1872) was the founder of New York City newspapers *The New Yorker* in 1934 and the *New York Tribune* in 1841. Newspapers of old often favored a particular political party; such was the case with Greeley's papers, which were Whig and later Republican Party newspapers. He was elected to one session of NYS legislature in 1848. In 1854 he transferred his allegiance to the newly formed Republican Party, which he helped form, and continued his antislavery editorials. In 1872 he attempted to run against Ulysses S. Grant in the new liberal Republican Party, but did not do well and died before the final results were tallied. Greeley's wife, Mary Young Cheney (1811–1872), whom he married in 1836, died a few months before he did. They had seven children, but only two daughters lived to adulthood.

The Horace Greeley House was the country home of the Greeley family from 1864 until 1873 and one of three homes that the Greeleys owned in Chappaqua.

The main floor consists of three primary rooms. The front parlor was used for formal entertaining and receiving guests. Over the handsome fireplace is a print that shows the Greeley family in 1872, the year that Greeley ran for president. The dining room, painted in a bright shade of red, overlooked Greeley's farm. On one wall a print shows Greeley's campaign slogan, "Yours for Universal amnesty and impartial suffrage." The music room is one of the rooms in the portion added by the Greeleys. This room includes a box pianoforte similar to the one belonging to the Greeleys. One portion of the current Research Room served as the butler's pantry.

The upper floor also consists of three primary historical rooms. When Greeley enlarged the house, he altered and modernized the second floor, transforming it from Federal to Victorian style. The family parlor was a more private sitting room than the downstairs parlor. In this room are displayed many items connected to Greeley's professional career and political activities. Horace Greeley's desk was in his New York Tribune office and remained in the Greeley family for many years, passing down through Greeley's daughter Gabrielle Greeley Clendenin. The girls' bedroom, shared by Gabrielle and Ida, is a bright and airy room, opening out onto a balcony through three French doors. The master bedroom is where Mary Greeley spent much of her time. The only photograph of her hangs on the wall by the door to the stairway. The meeting room behind the bedroom is part of the new section of the house and is a large room used for meetings and special exhibitions. This section of the house was added in the 1950s when the house was used as a gift shop.

The ground floor consists of a kitchen and laundry room. In the kitchen are several utilitarian objects such as a spinning wheel and yarn winder, which belonged to

Greeley's mother, and many other objects that one would find in a Victorian kitchen. Around the outside of the house are the kitchen, medicinal, and ornamental gardens.

The New Castle Historical Society bought the Greeley House in 1998, after it closed as a gift shop, and held a dedication in 2000.

Washington Irving's Sunnyside
3 W. Sunnyside Ln., Irvington; (914) 631-8200; hudsonvalley.org; open May through Nov; admission charged

This was the home of American author Washington Irving, best known for his short stories, such as "Rip Van Winkle" and "The Legend of Sleepy Hollow." Tour guides dressed in period costume lead you through the study, dining room, parlor, kitchen, and some of the bedrooms.

Washington Irving (1783–1859) was the last of eight children and said to be named after our first president, George Washington, whom he met when he was six years old.

One of the exciting things about Sunnyside is that it feels very much like a home; many of the objects displayed belonged either to Washington Irving or his family. Visitors especially enjoy seeing Irving's study, which remains as he would have kept it (his family left it largely intact after his death). All the furniture and most of the accessories on display belonged to him. The desk is a partner's desk, which means it allowed two people to work at it simultaneously. There's a porcelain paperweight with a spaniel on it that's rather darling, given to Irving by the poet William W. Waldron. Irving wrote to Waldron thanking him for the gift, saying, "You say it is intended to guard bank notes; if it can keep mine from vanishing it will prove a more effectual guard than any I have as yet set over there."

Truly, though, the entire home is charming, from one corner to the next. There are ever-changing views of the ten-acre grounds, surrounding landscape, and the Hudson River, and at one particular curve in the path, the cottage emerges into view. Irving paid tremendous attention to the development of the cottage and grounds, and visitors today encounter the space very much as Irving and his family would have.

"Few people today realize how prolific a writer Irving was and how popular he was in his time. Today we mainly know 'The Legend of Sleepy Hollow' and 'Rip Van Winkle,' but we forget his early satirical works or his travel essays and non-fiction writings. In fact, Irving's writings about the Alhambra in Granada, Spain, helped ensure that the palace was saved from destruction. There's actually a statue there in his honor. So while Irving helped make our region famous across the world, he had a huge influence beyond the banks of the Hudson River," says the marketing associate.

Irving often visited Herman Knickerbacker's home in Schaghticoke, New York, now known as the Knickerbocker Mansion museum (also included in this book). He published a major literary work, which was considered satirical, *A History of New York from the Beginning of the World to the End of the Dutch Dynasty*, in 1809 using the pseudonym Diedrich Knickerbocker. Irving was the first person to spell the name with an "o" in the third syllable, and it became so popular that the family adopted it permanently.

LONG ISLAND

Old Bethpage Village Restoration
1303 Round Swamp Rd., Old Bethpage; (516) 572-8401;
obvrnassau.com; open spring through Dec; admission charged

This is a living-history museum that allows visitors of all ages the ability to experience Long Island in the nineteenth century. The village is situated on 209 acres and consists of houses, barns, and buildings dating from 1660 through 1875.

"Old Bethpage Village Restoration boasts nineteen historic homes and over fifty historic structures. The differences in architecture, time periods, and the individual histories of the persons who lived there make these houses unique to the nineteenth-century Long Island "country" experience! Some of my most favorite artifacts at our site include an 1871 Omnibus, which originally operated as public transportation in Manhattan, as well as an antebellum safe that has moving rivets to detract from the location of the keyhole so as to make it more difficult to open. On our site is one of the first homes of renowned inventor Peter Cooper (though not often mentioned in normal history textbooks). Cooper was the founder of the Cooper Union Institute in Manhattan (a free higher-education center for mechanics,

engineering, and the arts). The Cooper Union is where Abraham Lincoln gave his infamous speech to win the nomination for the presidency. He is also credited with creating the first steam train in the United States, the 'Tom Thumb,' as well as a great many other patents and advancements furthering technology in this country," says the village manager.

Buildings in the complex (and where they were originally moved from) are Schenck House circa 1730 from Manhasset; Hewlett House circa 1795 from Woodbury; Dr. Searing House circa 1795 from Hempstead; Conklin House circa 1820 from Smithtown; Layton General Store built 1866 from East Norwich; Luyster circa 1820 from East Norwich; Noon Inn circa 1840 from East Meadow; Kirby House built 1839 in Hempstead; Benjamin House built 1829 in Northville; a schoolhouse built 1826 in Manhasset Valley Park; Manetto Hill Church built 1857 in Manetto Hill now Plainview; Blacksmith Shop circa 1875 from Hicksville; Hat Shop circa 1810 from Middle Island; Ritch House circa 1810 from Middle Island; Cooper House first section built 1600s then restored to circa 1815 from Hempstead; Lawrence House circa 1770 then restored to circa 1820 from College Point, Queens; Williams House circa 1820 then restored to circa 1860 from New Hyde Park; and Powell House first section built circa 1750 then restored to circa 1855, original to the property.

When perusing old newspapers on fultonhistory.com, I found that quite a few of the buildings, sometimes previously awaiting the wrecking ball, were moved to Old Bethpage Village Restoration in the mid-1960s. People must have been working like crazy to open the museum in 1970.

According to the May 24, 1967, edition of *Nassau Newsday*: "[A] hoist truck of the Long Island electrical firm of Broadway Maintenance Corp, was donated recently to provide aerial bucket for workmen to lift wires in the way of moving the 247-year-old Schenck House twenty-three miles from Manhasset to Old Bethpage where it'll become part of Nassau County Restoration Village."

Nassau Newsday featured the relocation project again on November 11, 1967: "The house once owned by Peter Cooper, designer of the first US steam locomotive, stands on the corner of Clinton and Front Streets, Hempstead, awaiting removal to Nassau County's Old Bethpage Village Restoration. Built in the seventeenth or early eighteenth century, the house will be restored to its nineteenth-century appearance by the county."

During your visit, knowledgeable costumed staff might be hammering in the blacksmith shop, putting the finishing touches on a gentleman's hat, sewing, knitting, making candles, shaping pottery, carpentry, tinsmithing, teaching in the one-room schoolhouse, churning butter, carding wool, or woodworking. Don't forget to stop by Powell's Farm and see an assortment of farm animals.

Old Westbury Gardens
71 Old Westbury Rd.; Old Westbury; (516) 333-0048; oldwestburygardens.org; open year-round; admission charged

This Charles II–style elegant mansion was completed in 1906 by English designer George A. Crawley for the John Shaffer Phipps family. The mansion sits within two hundred acres of formal gardens, landscaped grounds, woodlands, ponds, and lakes.

John "Jay" Shaffer Phipps (1874–1958), a lawyer, businessman, and heir to a US Steel fortune, married Margarita Grace (1876–1957) in 1903, and they had four children. This was the primary home for the Phipps family. Immediately following John's death, in 1959, his children opened the home to the public.

The entranceway into the estate is an experience within itself, lined with linden trees. Other garden areas are the Walled Garden, Rose Garden, and Lilac Walk; the Thatched Cottage, built for their only daughter, Peggy; West Pond; the Terraces of Westbury House; a colonnade and reflecting pool, South Lawn; and East Lake.

Westbury House is furnished with fine English antiques and decorative arts from the more than fifty years of the family's residence.

The mansion is entered through the magnificent front hall, which features a Bengal tiger, a souvenir trophy from the Phippses' honeymoon safari to India. Proceed through the mansion to Mrs. Phipps's study, which includes a wide assortment of books and a "hidden" closet that held Mr. Phipps's valuable violins. The ceiling in the West Porch is composed of steel beams covered in oak and hydraulic windows that were installed in the mid-1930s. Included in the White Drawing Room is a tea

table set with the Phippses' marvelous silver, some of which dates to the eighteenth century, and personal fine art of the Phipps children. The Red Ballroom was and still is a central location for gala entertainment and offers a spectacular view of the Grand Alée. The elegant dining room was originally designed by George Crawley for Henry Phipps's Fifth Avenue townhouse, but before the townhouse was demolished, the entire room including the ceiling, mantel, and wood paneling, was moved to Westbury House in 1924. Journey up to the second-floor hall and into the Adam Room guest bedroom, named after the late eighteenth-century English architect and interior designer, Robert Adam, whose artistry inspired George Crawley's design of this room. The master bedroom features portraits of the children and unobtrusive "jib" doors. Lastly is the Chippendale Bedroom decorated with hand-painted Chinese wallpaper displaying colorful birds and butterflies.

Fire Island Lighthouse Preservation Society
Burma Rd., Fire Island; (631) 661-4876; fireislandlighthouse.com; open year-round; admission charged

Discover what life was like as a lighthouse keeper and walk the 182 steps to the top of the tower for a great view. Smell the ocean air and experience Long Island's nautical history.

The first lighthouse built on Fire Island was lit in 1826 and was 74 feet high. This tower was not tall enough to be effective, so in 1857 Congress appropriated $40,000 for the construction of the 168-foot tower that you see today. It was first fitted with a first order Fresnel lens fueled by whale oil followed by lard and mineral oil, kerosene, and then electricity in 1938. In 1973 it was decommissioned, then it was reinstated as an official aid to navigation again in 1986. The Fire Island Lighthouse Preservation Society (FLIPS) got involved in 1996 and assumed ownership and maintenance from the US Coast Guard in 2006.

Photos and displays tell the story of life at the Fire Island Lighthouse and about the group of Long Islanders who raised the funds to restore the historic site.

Exhibit areas include two floors of interactive exhibits in the Keeper's Quarters, the Len's Building to view the first order Fresnel lens that was up in the tower from

1858 to 1933, and the Boathouse to examine an authentic surf boat and equipment used by the US Life-Saving Service.

The Whaling Museum & Education Center
302 Main St., Cold Spring Harbor; (631) 367-3418; cshwhalingmuseum.org; open year-round; admission charged

Learn about a Long Island industry that was second only to farming in the mid-1800s. Discover the history of whaling on Long Island, and view a nineteenth-century whaleboat at this family-friendly museum.

Exhibit areas are "Thar She Blows: Whaling History on Long Island," "If I Were a Whaler," "Scrimshaw & Whalebone Art," "Diorama of Cold Spring Harbor circa 1850," and "Folk Art."

"My favorite artifact is our whaleboat. Whale ships would typically carry about three to five whaleboats on board. These small boats would be used to pursue and kill whales once they were spotted from the main ship. Standing next to our whaleboat gives you such an incredible opportunity to imagine yourself out in the middle of the ocean, hunting one of the largest animals to ever live. It's truly humbling. Our whaleboat was used on the brig *Daisy* on one of the last American whaling voyages

(1912–1913) and is the only one of its kind on display with its original gear in New York. Many tourists are surprised to learn that there were women who went on whaling voyages. The captain of a whaling ship had the option of bringing his wife and family along. These women often struggled with the long and uncomfortable voyages, but many of them also relished the opportunity to visit faraway places and learn new skills. We have tried to tell some of their stories in our exhibits. Another artifact I love is an orca (killer whale) skull we have on display. This particular orca beached itself in Orient Point, Long Island, in 1944. The skull is in fairly good condition, save for the teeth, some of which were sawed off by souvenir hunters as it lay on the beach. Back in 1944, the head of this beached whale was acquired by Charles Davenport, one of the founders of the Whaling Museum. He planned to render the flesh from the bones so that the museum would be able to display the skull. Typically, this would be done by submerging the skull in a pond, where it would be left to macerate slowly. Davenport was impatient and instead chose to boil it in a shed in the dead of winter. He caught a cold, developed pneumonia, and died before he could see the skull on display," says the curator of education.

NEW YORK CITY

Edgar Allan Poe Cottage
2640 Grand Concourse at E. Kingsbridge Rd., New York City

Museum of Bronx History
3266 Bainbridge Ave., New York City; (718) 881-8900;
bronxhistoricalsociety.org; open year-round; admission charged

The Bronx County Historical Society, which began in 1955, oversees the Edgar Allan Poe Cottage and the Museum of Bronx History.

The Edgar Allan Poe Cottage was the former home, built in 1812, of Edgar Allan Poe, American author, and is situated in the Fordam neighborhood of Poe Park.

Edgar Allan Poe (1809–1849) was best known for his poetry and short stories, in particular his tales of mystery and the macabre. Poe married Virginia Eliza Clemm (1822–1847) in 1836, and they moved to the cottage in Fordam in 1846. Poe rented the house from John Valentine for $100 per year. Between 1846 and 1849 Poe wrote "Annabel Lee," "The Bells" and "Ulalume." After Poe's death the house had many owners until New York City bought it in 1913, moved it across the street, and opened it as a museum in 1917. The Bronx County Historical Society has administered the Edgar Allan Poe Cottage as a historic house museum since 1975, in cooperation with the New York City Department of Parks & Recreation and the Historic House Trust of New York City.

"As far as artifacts go, one of the most interesting in Poe Cottage is the mirror hanging on the wall in the first floor. It is the only object that might have belonged to Poe himself. The rest of the furniture in the cottage is period, though probably did not belong to Poe. The bed, I've been told, possibly belonged to Poe's dying wife, but I do not think there's definitive confirmation of that. Story has it that the person who owned the cottage, before it was set aside as a historical monument in the early twentieth century, was a dentist, so the blood and screams likely coming from the cottage were a fitting monument to Poe's macabre tales in my mind. We have a very large collection of artifacts under the aegis of the Museum of Bronx History— everything ranging from early colonial documents from the area to beer paraphernalia (the Bronx had a booming brewing business during the late nineteenth and early twentieth centuries) and much more," says the librarian/archivist.

The Museum of Bronx History is housed in the Valentine-Varian house, built in 1758, and offers exhibits in three galleries. This Georgian vernacular–style house is the second-oldest house in the Bronx.

The house was originally built on 260 acres of land by Isaac Valentine. Amazingly the house, which was a headquarters for Hessian troops for a time, survived battles fought during the Revolution then was sold to Isaac Varian in 1792. Members of the Varian family lived in the house until it was sold to William F. Beller in 1905. William C. Beller, son of William F., donated the house to the Bronx County Historical Society in 1965 and paid to move the house across the street. The Valentine-Varian house opened as a museum in 1968.

Old Stone House
336 3rd St., Brooklyn; (718) 768-3195; theoldstonehouse.org; open year-round; admission by donation

The Old Stone House (OSH) building, located in Washington Park, is a reconstruction of the Vechte-Cortelyou Dutch farmhouse that was built in 1699. It was destroyed in 1897 then reconstructed with some of the original stones in 1933 to 1934. The house was also a clubhouse for the Brooklyn Superbas baseball team, predecessors of the Brooklyn Dodgers.

Excerpts from an article about the Old Stone House published in the December 11, 1887, *Brooklyn Daily Eagle* describe the house as "[t]he first house on the line of the road beyond First Street, at the commencement of the century, as it is now, was the Cortelyou or Vechte house. It used to be known as '1699' from iron figures secured to the west gable next to the road, but these figures were removed by unknown parties about 30 years ago. Claes Adriaenetse Van Vetchten, an emigrant from Holland settled on and owned the plantation. . . . In 1790 Nicholas R. Cowenhoven, grandson of Nicholas Vechte, sold it to Jacques Cortelyou who resided in it until 1804. . . . The house now stands in the Northeast corner of Washington Park (the baseball grounds). The old Vechte house is now used as a costume house for the baseballists."

"We love that the Old Stone House is located in the center of an active park that includes references to the Battle of Brooklyn and OSH's agricultural past in the playground equipment. We also have an acre of lovely gardens with native and useful plants. All this helps make a relevant link to the site's history. We think the most popular element of our exhibit is 'Take the Hill'—an interactive Battle of Brooklyn game. Most people are not aware that one in three Brooklynites was enslaved at the time of the American Revolution," says the executive director.

A permanent exhibit is "The Old Stone House: Witness to War—An Exhibit Exploring the Battle of Brooklyn and the Occupation." The exhibit takes visitors on a journey through the Revolutionary War era in Brooklyn from 1776 to 1783.

The Battle of Brooklyn, also known as the Battle of Long Island, because the land was in western Long Island at the time, was fought on August 27, 1776, and was the first major battle since the patriots declared independence on July 4. The battle did not go well for the Continental Army, as the British won and held on to the Port of New York until the end of the war in 1783.

Old Stone House is also the conservancy organization for JJ Byrne Playground and Washington Park.

New York Transit Museum
99 Schermerhorn St., Brooklyn; (718) 694-1600; nytransitmuseum.org; admission charged

Explore a selection of rotating and long-term exhibits pertaining to mass transportation in New York City. Visitors can board the vintage cars, sit at the wheel of a city bus, step through a time tunnel of turnstiles, and explore changing exhibits that highlight the cultural, social, and technological history of mass transit.

"My favorite aspect of the New York Transit Museum is the underground 1936 subway station home that spans a full city block (a New York City block is about 260 feet long)," says the museum's director. "The Court Street Station was only active for ten years, but it's connected to the rest of the subway system, enabling us to take our vintage fleet of subway cars out on the very rails they were designed for. There is something incredible about riding a 1904 wooden carriage subway car through a

stretch of elevated tracks in Brooklyn or taking a 1917 IRT car up to Yankee Stadium. We have a unique ability to be a museum without walls and to meet people where they are. The folks who come to the museum have often heard through the grapevine that we are an interesting place. At some level, I suppose most folks understand that the subway and mass transit shaped New York, but once you come to the Transit Museum, you truly walk away knowing that New York is New York because of mass transit. It is such a fun thing to watch people leave and say "I had no idea! And I'll be back!"

The "Ticket to Ride" exhibit shows the evolution of fare collection across all of New York's modes of transportation. Visitors can see and touch equipment such as turnstiles and fare boxes, and get a sense of the fare collection process. "Steel, Stone & Backbone: Building New York's Subways" presents a look at the construction methods and labor required to build the city's first subway line at the turn of the twentieth century. Historic artifacts, video footage, and photography bring to life the dedication and tenacity of the workers who made this project possible. "Moving the Millions" highlights the evolution of the subway and the major issues and events that influenced the development of the largest transportation network in North America. "On the Streets: New York's Trolleys and Buses" tells the story of aboveground mobility and surface transit from the early 1800s to the present. A twelve-seat city bus, a "fishbowl" bus cab, walk/don't walk signs, parking meters, fire hydrants, traffic lights, and an array of other interactive "street furniture" bring this exhibit to life. The Dr. George T. F. Rahilly (1916–2002) Trolley and Bus Study Center features over fifty detailed scale models of trolleys and work cars, with a focus on Brooklyn.

Vintage cars and buses on display are the BMT Q Car Number 1612C (1908, rebuilt 1938), in service 1908–1969; BRT Brooklyn Union Elevated Car Number 1407 (1907), in service 1908–1969; IRT R-15 Car Number 6239 (1950), in service 1950–1985; IRT R-12 Car Number 5760 (1948), in service 1948–1985; R-11 Prototype/R-34 Car Number 8013 (1949), in service 1949–1976; IRT R-17 Car Number 6609 (1955), in service 1955–1986; IND R-1 "City-Car" Number 100 (1930), in service 1931–1970; Bus Number 3100 (1956), the first air-conditioned bus; Bus Number 236 (1980); Bus Number 2969 (1948); Bus Number 3865 (1993); Bus Number 100 (1959); Bus Number 621 (1979); Bus Number 3006 (1988); Bus Number 1502 (1982); Bus Number 5227 (1971, rebuilt 1985); Bus Number 1201 (1981), and Bus Number 8928 (1968).

Museum of Jewish Heritage
36 Battery Place, New York City; (646) 437-4202; mjhnyc.org; open year-round; admission charged

A living memorial, the Museum of Jewish Heritage depicts Jewish life before, during, and after the Holocaust.

Here is a brief timeline of the Holocaust that begins in 1933 when Adolf Hitler becomes chancellor of Germany, the first concentration camp is established in Dachau, Germany, and the Nazis boycott all Jewish businesses in Germany. In 1936 the Olympics take place in Berlin, and Germany forms military pacts with Italy and Japan. The next year the Buchenwald concentration camp is created, and in 1938 passports of German Jews are marked with a "J." In 1939 the euthanasia (T4) program and World

War II begins, and Jewish ghettos are set up in Poland. Germany continues to invade countries, and the Auschwitz concentration camp opens in 1940. In 1941 Jewish ghettos in Poland are sealed, the first experimental gassing take place in Auschwitz, and the United States enters World War II. In 1942 Balzec and other extermination camps begin, and in 1943 the Jews start the Warsaw ghetto uprising. In 1944 Hungary registers Jews, D-Day (invasion of Normandy) takes place, and the Auschwitz-Birkenau uprising occurs. Allied forces begin liberating concentration camps, Germany surrenders on May 7, 1945, and the Nuremberg Trials begin.

Visitors to the museum can explore documents, textiles, Judaica, toys, musical instruments, diaries and memoirs, posters, and other visual materials. Some of the items you might see include treasured and irreplaceable family photographs, heirloom Sabbath candlesticks, a wedding present of wooden clogs, and a tin Hanukkah menorah with seventeen candleholders so that two families could share it for the holiday. These objects illustrate Jewish life, reveal Jewish self-reliance in the face of exclusion, and suggest the pain of extreme loss in the Shoah.

I will never forget my first real-life experience with the Holocaust, which took place in the area of 42nd Street in Manhattan about forty-five years ago when I was twenty-something. It was a shopping day trip for my boss, who referred to the area as the "jewelry district," to buy silversmith supplies. We stopped at a coffee shop for a snack, and I noticed that the older lady who served us had numbers tattooed on her forearm. I asked my boss, who happened to be of the Jewish faith, what the numbers were all about, and he told me that she had spent time in a concentration camp. Reading about the Holocaust in books is one thing; seeing those tattooed numbers is quite another realization.

Visiting the Museum of Jewish Heritage and seeing photos and artifacts up close is a much better way to get a real feel for the years 1933 to 1945.

National 9/11 Memorial & Museum
180 Greenwich St., New York City; (212) 312-8800; 911memorial.org; open year-round; admission charged

This memorial and museum remembers and honors the 2,977 people killed in the horrific attacks of September 11, 2001, and the six killed on February 26, 1993. The museum tells the story of 9/11 through artifacts, imagery, personal stories, and interactive technology. Learn about the attacks through core exhibitions, special exhibitions, and rotating galleries in the museum's 110,000 square feet of space. Visitors learn how the normalcy of a beautiful day was overtaken by a sense of shock, disbelief, and increasing horror as America came under attack.

The World Trade Center Twin Towers complex, which sat on sixteen acres, was dedicated on April 4, 1973. The Twin Towers were 110-story skyscrapers standing

1,368- and 1,362-feet-tall, the tallest buildings in the world. On the morning of September 11, 2001, a total of nineteen terrorists prepared to hijack four California-bound commercial airlines shortly after their departures from airports in Boston, Massachusetts; Newark, New Jersey; and Washington, DC. Flight 11 hit the North Tower of the World Trade Center at 8:46 a.m., Flight 175 hit the South Tower at 9:03 a.m., Flight 77 crashed into the Pentagon at 9:37 a.m., and Flight 93 crashed into a field in Shanksville, Pennsylvania, at 10:03 a.m. The South Tower collapsed at 9:59 a.m. and the North Tower at 10:28 a.m.

The bombing of the World Trade Center on February 26, 1993, took place at 12:18 p.m. The explosion, detonated in the garage, created a five-story, 150-foot-wide crater filled with four thousand tons of rubble in the subgrade levels of the towers and undermined the floor of an adjoining hotel. The terrorist attack killed six people, and more than one thousand people were injured, including eighty-eight firefighters, thirty-five police officers, and an emergency medical services worker. About fifty thousand people evacuated from the WTC complex.

All visitors are able to experience the introductory exhibits on the ramp, the Survivors Stairs and Memorial Hall, Tribute Walk, South Tower Excavation, North Tower Excavation, "K-9 Courage," "In Memoriam," the historical exhibition, Center Passage, Foundation Hall, the Atrium, the Auditorium, "Reflecting on 9/11," "Rebirth at Ground Zero" and "Revealed: The Hunt for Bin Laden."

The historical exhibition presents the story of 9/11 using artifacts, images, first-person testimony, and archival audio and video recordings. The exhibition is made up of three parts: the "Events of the Day," as they unfolded; "Before 9/11," which provides the historical context leading up to the attacks; and "After 9/11," which addresses the immediate aftermath and ongoing repercussions of the terrorist attacks. "Memorial Exhibition: Memoriam" honors the 2,977 individuals killed as a result of the terrorist attacks of September 11, 2001, at this site as well as at the Pentagon and in Somerset County, Pennsylvania. It also honors the six individuals killed in the terrorist bombing of the World Trade Center on February 26, 1993. "Revealed: The Hunt for Bin Laden" examines the intelligence and military activities that led to a compound in Abbottabad, Pakistan, where Osama bin Laden was killed nearly ten years after 9/11. "K-9 Courage" honors the hundreds of dogs that participated in the response to the 9/11 attacks.

Outside, the museum's memorial pools stand in the footprints of the Twin Towers. Each pool is one acre in size. There are 413 swamp white oak trees on the memorial plaza and one callery pear tree, known as the "Survivor Tree." The callery pear tree became known as the Survivor Tree because it survived severe damage at Ground Zero. It was removed from the rubble and rehabilitated by the New York City Department of Parks & Recreation, then returned to the memorial in 2010 with new, smooth limbs extending from the gnarled stumps.

The 9/11 Memorial Glade is an outdoor pathway flanked by six stone monoliths pointed skyward that symbolize strength and determination through adversity in honor of those who are sick or who have died from exposure to toxins in the aftermath of the 9/11 attacks. The glade was dedicated on May 30, 2019, the eighteenth anniversary of the formal end of recovery operations at Ground Zero.

Louis Armstrong House Museum
34-56 107th St., Queens; (718) 478-8274; louisarmstronghouse.org; open year-round for guided tours; admission charged

The legacy of legendary jazz instrumentalist and vocalist Louis Armstrong is preserved at this museum.

Louis Daniel Armstrong (1901–1971), nicknamed "Satchmo," was best known for his trumpet playing, but he was also a composer, vocalist, and actor. He bought his first cornet in 1907 with a loan from his employer, the Karnofsky family, and made his first recording with the King Oliver's Creole Jazz Band in 1923. He had a rather tumultuous upbringing in New Orleans, then settled in Queens in 1943, where he remained until his death. Armstrong was married a few times but never had any children.

An advertisement published in the August 11, 1966, *The Wave*, Rockaway Beach, New York, read: "Nightly Incl. Sun. at 8:30 thru Sept. 4 tickets $5, $4, $3, $2 – 'Best Daily Double In Town' Guy Lombardo presents Louis Armstrong in the

Musical Spectacular Mardi Gras! Guy Lombardo and his Royal Canadians – Free Dancing After the Show – Louis Armstong's & Guy Lombardo's Bands – For nearest ticket office call: (516) CA 1- 3103 – Jones Beach Theater."

Satchmo's numerous achievements include developing a way of playing jazz as an instrumentalist and vocalist; recording hit songs for five decades; writing two autobiographies; appearing in more than thirty films; composing dozens of songs, and performing an average of three hundred concerts each year in all parts of the world.

Some of Satchmo's top hits are "What a Wonderful World," "La Vie En Rose," "A Kiss to Build a Dream On," "When You're Smiling," "When the Saints Go Marching In," "That Lucky Old Sun," "Jeepers Creepers," "Mack the Knife," "St. James Infirmary," and "Hello Dolly."

Collections at the museum are many. The Satchmo Collection is a steadily growing collection of Armstrong-related materials donated to the museum by Armstrong friends, fans, and collectors. Highlights include a 1934 Selmer trumpet and mouthpiece given to Louis by King George V of England, a cornet case autographed by Louis and donated by trumpet player Randy Sandke, and two scrapbooks compiled by longtime Armstrong bassist Arvell Shaw.

The Louis Armstrong House Collection contains all the furniture, appliances, paintings, decorations, and other objects left in the house after Louis and Lucille's deaths. Other collections are the Louis Armstrong Collection, Institutional History Collection, Jack Bradley Collection, Phoebe Jacobs Collection, Gosta Hagglof Collection, Robert G. Hilbert Collection, Ernie Anderson Collection, Winfried Maier Collection, and Jay Anderson Collection.

Exhibits include "Satchmo's Stuff," which features the best and most interesting artifacts from the collections, including Armstrong's gold-plated trumpet, manuscripts, photos, clothing, and a sample of some of the collage work that Louis created in his spare time. The exhibit "That's My Home: 75 years of the Armstrongs in Corona" explores the Armstrongs' history in Corona, with many rare photographs taken by photographers such as Burt Goldblatt, Paul Studer, John Loengard, Jack Bradley, and Charles Graham. Many of these images have never been previously exhibited.

My dad always played assorted jazz artists' songs on the record player, and even as a kid I could always tell when a Louis Armstrong song was playing because of his distinctive raspy voice. I listened to his songs on YouTube while writing this entry.

The Vander-Ende Onderdonk House
1820 Flushing Ave., Ridgewood; (718) 456-1778; onderdonkhouse.org; open year-round; admission charged

Visit the oldest Dutch Colonial stone house in New York City, built in 1709 by the Vander-Endes.

Peter Stuyvesant granted the land it sits on in the mid-seventeenth century, and by 1660, Hendrick Barents Smidt occupied a small house on the site, then referred to as a plantation. In 1709, Paulus Vander Ende of Flatbush purchased the farm and began construction of the current house. During the 1820s, Adrian Onderdonk erected a small frame addition to the stone house immediately above the remnants of the foundation of the 1660 building. The Greater Ridgewood Historical Society was established in 1975 by a group of local residents to prevent the demolition of the Vander-Ende Onderdonk House. They bought the property in 1976 then raised funds for six years to reconstruct the house, which had been seriously damaged by a fire in 1975.

"Onderdonk House really speaks for itself; it is a testament to the local community who saved the house from the bulldozer and eventually restored it for public programs. It represents over three hundred years of local history: as part of the homeland of the Mespaetches Tribe, to the Dutch farmers, through the industrial era to post-war commercialization, and finally as a historic site and museum. The Vander-Ende Onderdonk House, where history meets community! Most tourists are amazed to find the grounds in the middle of an industrial and commercial area of Ridgewood. It is an oasis of gardens, trees, and open space on two acres," says a board member.

"We love some of our Dutch documents and primary documents from the Onderdonks, most agreed that the bottles and glass left from the first commercial business in the Onderdonk House after the farm was sold and subdivided are our favorite artifacts. This includes some rare bottles and stained glass. These items were recovered during archaeological investigations but we also just find pieces that percolate up in our gardens and lawns," says the board member docents.

Snug Harbor Cultural Center & Botanical Garden
1000 Richmond Terrace, Staten Island; (718) 425-3504; snug-harbor.org; open year-round; admission charged

Five museums in one offer history, maritime collections, art, and more in Staten Island.

Snug Harbor is a place where history, architecture, visual and performing arts, gardens, agriculture, and education come together and provide dynamic experiences for all ages. Snug Harbor is also home to the Newhouse Center for Contemporary Art, Snug Harbor Artist Residency Program (SHARP), Staten Island Museum, Staten Island Children's Museum, Noble Maritime Collection, Art Lab, Children's Harbor Montessori School, and Staten Island Conservatory of Music.

Snug Harbor was founded with the execution of the will of Robert Richard Randall (1750–1801), heir to a shipping fortune, who often prefaced his name with "Captain." His will was supposedly drawn up right before his death by Alexander Hamilton. The will required the family fortune and his Minto Farm estate be used to build and operate a haven for "aged, decrepit, and worn-out sailors." It opened to sailors in 1831.

An article about the founder's monument was published in the May 11, 1884, *Brooklyn Daily Eagle*: "The statue of Robert Richard Randall, the founder of Sailor's Snug Harbor at West Brighton, made by M. Saint Gaudens will be unveiled at that place on Decoration Day." The statute still stands today.

Over the next century, Sailors' Snug Harbor expanded from its original three buildings to fifty structures and nine hundred residents from every corner of the world.

By the turn of the twentieth century, Sailors' Snug Harbor was a self-sustaining community with farms, a dairy, a bakery, workshops, a power plant, a chapel, a sanatorium, a hospital, a concert hall, dormitories, recreation areas, gardens, a cemetery, and unlimited funds. In the mid-twentieth century the number of residents dwindled because other programs such as Social Security came into play, the Randall endowment started to run out, and the historic buildings began to deteriorate. In 1975 the not-for-profit Snug Harbor Cultural Center was formed to operate the buildings, and the Staten Island Botanical Gardens managed the gardens. The two organizations merged in 2008 to form Snug Harbor Cultural Center & Botanical Garden.

The Staten Island Museum's permanent collections contain natural science specimens, archival records, and works of art and design that represents Staten Island's natural and cultural history across time.

The Noble Maritime Collection features the work of John A. Noble (1913–1983), the maritime artist who chronicled the last chapter in the Age of Sail. Permanent exhibit areas include the Ship Model Gallery, Noble's Houseboat Studio, the Writing Room, the Dormitory Room, and the "Noble Crew Exhibition," dedicated to John A. Santore, who was killed at the World Trade Center on September 11, 2001.

In October the center offers special Ghost Tours in the Governor's House and Matron's House, buildings that are usually closed to the public and have a history of unexplained phenomena.

The Jacques Marchais Museum of Tibetan Art
338 Lighthouse Ave., Staten Island; (718) 987-3500; tibetanmuseum.org; open year-round; admission charged

Home to one of the United States' most extensive collections of Himalayan and Tibetan artifacts, the Jacques Marchais Museum is nestled into the side of Lighthouse Hill. The rustic complex of fieldstone buildings resembles a Tibetan mountain monastery. Outside the buildings is the Samadi Garden, which features a fishpond, meditation cells, and many plants native to the Himalayas.

Jacques Marchais Coblentz (1887–1948) was born in Cincinnati, Ohio. Her father gave her a male name before she was born and then never changed it to the female version, Jacqueline. She settled in Staten Island with her second husband, Harry Klauber (1885–1948), in 1921 and began collecting Tibetan art, which became a lifelong activity. She ended up collecting over one thousand objects including sculptures, ritual objects, musical instruments, thangkas (scroll paintings), and furniture. Marchais decided to offer her collection to the public in 1947 and sadly died a few months after the opening.

The collections also include Himalayan artifacts donated by Ambassador Phillip R. Trimble, the US ambassador to Nepal from 1980 to 1981; Tibetan and Nepalese artifacts acquired by Dr. Walter Meuly in the 1960s and 1970s and donated by his grandson Jeremy Leavitt; and Zan Pars Tibetan ritual objects donated by Bill Jones of Paris, France.

Special programs throughout the year include films, musical performances, lectures and travel talks, traditional Tibetan crafts, and family activities.

Frank Lloyd Wright's Martin House
125 Jewett Pkwy., Buffalo; (877) 377-3858; martinhouse.org; open year-round; admission charged

Take a tour of the unique house that architect Frank Lloyd Wright (1867–1959) built for wealthy businessman Darwin D. Martin (1865–1935) during the years 1903 to 1905. An assortment of tours are offered, including guided, self-guided, landscape, and twilight.

"Fireplaces are a prominent feature in a Wright-designed home, and the central four-sided Wisteria Mosaic Fireplace inside the Martin House is truly a masterpiece. One of the most ambitious from Wright's Prairie house period, this hearth served as a canvas for an elaborately decorated work of art consisting of thousands of individual glass tiles in a warm palette of bronzes, golds, and greens. It is a naturalistic depiction of wisteria branches, leaves, and blossoms, and it's simply stunning. Visitors are often surprised by the magnitude of the estate, which is composed of six interconnected buildings including the main Martin House, a pergola, a conservatory, a carriage house, the Barton House, and a gardener's cottage. Over the years, some of these structures suffered severe damage while others were demolished. Today's visitors are astonished by the detailed stories of the restoration and reconstruction of the estate," says the marketing manager.

Frank Lloyd Wright designed some fifty-five pieces of furniture for the Martin House commission. The collection includes quarter-sawn oak tables, chairs and couches, built-in cabinetry with art glass doors, and massive bronze firewood boxes. Perhaps most notable is Wright's iconic barrel chair, first designed for the Martin House and later adapted by the architect for a number of his other projects. The

Martin House estate contains 394 Frank Lloyd Wright–designed panels of art glass, or "light screens," as the architect liked to call them. Other highlights of the museum collection include an eclectic array of architectural fragments, books, photographs, and ephemera related to the Martin House, the Martin family, or Frank Lloyd Wright in general.

A tour of the Martin House offers a glimpse into its rich history, its significance to the city of Buffalo, and the influence Wright continues to have on architecture, art, and design.

Theodore Roosevelt Inaugural Site
641 Delaware Ave., Buffalo; (716) 884-0095; trsite.org; open year-round; admission charged

Imagine what Vice President Theodore Roosevelt was thinking when President William McKinley is shot on September 6, 1901, and eight days later, following McKinley's death, Roosevelt takes the oath of office as the twenty-sixth president of the United States of America on September 14, 1901, in a private home in Buffalo, New York. Guided tours will walk you through the inauguration and Theodore Roosevelt's ("TR's") presidency.

Theodore Roosevelt was born in New York City on October 27, 1858, the second child of Theodore and Martha "Mittie" (Bulloch) Roosevelt. He graduated from Harvard in 1880 and shortly afterward married his college sweetheart, Alice Hathaway Lee. Roosevelt won his first political office as a NYS assemblyman in 1881. The year 1884 brought about a happy occasion with the birth of his daughter Alice, but sadness followed when his wife and mother died a couple of days after the birth. Overwhelmed with the deaths, he left his daughter with his sister Alice and went out to the Dakota Territory for a couple of years. In 1886 Roosevelt married Edith Kermit Carow, and they had five children. Public service came about again in 1889 when he was appointed US Civil Service commissioner, then president of the New York City Police Board in 1895 and assistant secretary of the Navy in 1897. When the Spanish-American War began in 1898, Roosevelt led a cavalry regiment named the Rough Riders in Cuba. Immediately following the war he became NYS's thirty-third governor from 1899 to 1900, then vice president under William McKinley.

From 1838 to 1846 the museum was one of the buildings in the Buffalo or Poinsett Barracks then it had private owners until 1880. The Wilcox family owned the home from 1883 to 1933. The next owners were Oliver and Kathryn Lawrence, who operated a restaurant in it from 1938 to 1961. The house fell into disrepair until 1966 when it was granted national historic status and allocated funds for restoration. In 1971 the doors were opened to the public.

"Why did the inauguration take place in a private home? TR and the home's resident, Ansley Wilcox, a prominent Buffalo attorney, served on two New York State commissions dealing with civil service and public lands during TR's days in the NYS Assembly. When Roosevelt came to Buffalo after the shooting of President William McKinley, it was natural for him to stay in the home of his good friend. TR's swearing-in ceremony in Buffalo, New York, was one of only four times in American history when a president took the oath of office outside the nation's capital. Another little-known fact about the TR swearing in was that there was no Bible and the words, 'so help me God,' were not spoken by Roosevelt; it is not constitutionally required. Finally, in TR's haste to return to Buffalo from the family camping trip he was on in New York's Adirondack Mountains, he arrived in Buffalo in camping attire and had to borrow a frock coat and pants for the swearing-in ceremony," says the executive director.

The museum offers a combination of historically restored rooms and interactive exhibits. The Orientation Room draws you into the year 1901 and the celebration of the Pan-American Exposition (a world's fair of sorts). Historic rooms place you where the inauguration unfolded. Hear what TR might have been thinking moments before becoming president in the Issues Theater. The second floor of the TR site is a testament to TR's enduring legacy. Compare issues that TR faced in the early 1900s to those of today.

"We have the actual desk that Theodore Roosevelt used when he established an office during his stay here. Most notably he used the desk to write his first presidential

proclamation. Under normal circumstances, a newly inaugurated president would give an inaugural address, but the tragic nature of Theodore Roosevelt's swearing-in required a different tone. TR used his proclamation to honor President McKinley's life and express his commitment to fulfilling McKinley's platform for the remainder of the term. The key to the Temple of Music, which was a temporary building constructed for the Pan-American Exposition in 1901 and was where President McKinley was shot. One of the young surgical assistants kept the needle used during President McKinley's surgery because of its significance, and ultimately it found its way into our collection," says the development and communications manager.

Holland Land Office Museum
131 W. Main St., Batavia; (585) 343-4727; hollandlandoffice.com; open year-round; admission charged

Learn about the types of equipment used to survey land in the early 1800s; Joseph Ellicott (1760–1826), surveyor for the Holland Land Company; and an executioner's gibbet (gallows).

"A favorite aspect of the museum is that we are located in the original building that housed the Holland Land Office. The structure was built in 1815 and was responsible for the vast majority of sales of land in the western New York area. The Holland Land Company was responsible for 3.25 million acres, and all of the sales of that land came through our building, along with many of the settlers and purchasers. Being housed in this building really drives home the point that we are the 'Birthplace of Western New York.' The most common 'wow' moment is when visitors make the connection of the Holland Land Company to their own property deeds. For many of them the Holland Land Company is the first owner listed on their deeds. It brings it full circle as they step foot in the place where their land came from, and it becomes very personal and relatable, bringing the connection to their local history even closer," says the executive director.

Exhibits include "Joseph Ellicott and the Holland Land Company," which features his desk and a model of the ship *The Batavia*; "Native Americans in Western New York," with a 3D model of a longhouse; "Pioneer Kitchen," where you can feel for yourself how heavy a cast-iron pot is; "Tour of Batavia," where you will see an old post office; and "Military History of Genesee County," from the Revolution to the Vietnam War.

Some of the executive director's favorite artifacts include a Medal of Honor awarded to Charles Rand, the calling card collection of General Emory Upton, and an executioner's gibbet. Rand was a Civil War soldier from Batavia, whose heroics that led to him being awarded the Medal of Honor are some of the earliest in its history. Upton was a Batavia native who fought in the Civil War and eventually became a general. He was at the forefront of many of the reforms meant to modernize the

US Army during and after the war. The collection contains fifty-six signatures from some very famous individuals including Robert E. Lee, Ulysses S. Grant, Brigham Young, James Longstreet, and Ralph Waldo Emerson, among many others. The Genesee County gibbet was used to execute prisoners by hanging at the first Genesee County jail.

LeRoy House and Jell-O Gallery
23 E. Main St., LeRoy; (585) 768-7433; leroyhistoricalsociety.org; open year-round; admission charged

Gelatin was around in the early 1800s, but LeRoy is the birthplace of the "Jell-O" trademark and future marketing of the sweet product in 1897. After visiting the Jell-O Gallery, stroll down the Jell-O Brick Road to the LeRoy House/Museum. Both museums are maintained by the LeRoy Historical Society.

The LeRoy House recounts the timeline of the town of LeRoy from about 1820 to 1920. It was the first home of Jacob LeRoy, who was the land agent for the eighty-six-thousand-acre Triangle Tract in the 1820s. In addition to the story of the LeRoy family, there is the story of Ingham University, the first university for women to grant a four-year degree. Reverend Samuel Cox, a noted abolitionist, lived in the house during the 1850s while serving as chancellor of the university. Exhibit areas include the children's room with "hands-on" activities, the Morganville Pottery room, the transportation room housing carriages to automobiles, a 1930s kitchen with a special display of lime jello, and a boardinghouse room from the 1880s.

An interesting display in the LeRoy House is a miniature painting of Senator Henry Clay on the Senate floor. The original was seven by eleven feet and painted by LeRoy native Phineas Staunton in 1865. It was displayed in assorted places in LeRoy until the LeRoy Historical Society donated it to America in 2010, where it is on display in the Senate wing of the US Capitol.

In 1897, Pearle Wait, a carpenter in LeRoy, was experimenting with gelatin and came up with a fruit-flavored dessert that his wife May named Jell-O. He attempted to market his product but lacked capital and experience, so Wait sold the trademark to Orator Frank Woodward in 1899 for $450. Sales were not going well, so Woodward sold the business to Sam Nico for $35. In 1900 the Jell-O name was first used by the Genesee Pure Food Company. Sales skyrocketed to $250,000 in the year 1902.

The following Jell-O advertisement was published in the November 17, 1902, edition of the *Albany Evening Journal*: "What Shall We Have for Dessert? This question arises in the family every day. Let us answer it to-day. Try Jell-O, a delicious and healthful dessert. Prepared in two minutes. No boiling! No baking! Add boiling water and set to cool. Flavors: Lemon, Orange, Raspberry and Strawberry. Get a package at your grocers to-day, 10 cts."

Elizabeth King became the "Jell-O Girl" in 1904. In 1923 the Jell-O Company Inc. was organized and took over the entire assets of the Genesee Pure Foods Company with no change in management. In 1934 General Foods signed Jack Benny to advertise Jell-O on the radio and the world came to know "J-E-L-L-O." Jell-O was one of LeRoy's most important industries until it closed in 1964. Today Jell-O is manufactured by Kraft/General Foods in Dover, Delaware.

The director told me about some of the interesting memorabilia in the Jell-O Gallery, which is housed in the Academic building, built in 1898: the "wall of 100 molds," 1920s oil paintings that were used for magazine ads, Jell-O Barbie, the Jell-O arch that was on display at the Salt Lake City Olympics, EEG machine results of Jell-O and brain waves, and a gelometer, which is used to measure the strength of gelatin. The gelometer was featured on *To Tell the Truth* when the director appeared on the TV show. Canadian visitors like to look for the hockey puck Jell-O mold and the box that says "Canada's Most Famous Dessert." Probably the most photographed object is a huge cow with an image of the Jell-O girl on the side with fruit on her face.

The LeRoy Historical Society also offers a map of their Barn Quilt Trail.

Herschell Carrousel Factory Museum
180 Thompson St., North Tonawanda; (716) 693-1885; carrouselmuseum.org; open year-round; admission charged

This museum is perfect for families with children, as it offers history and fun all rolled up into one.

"The Herschell Carrousel Factory Museum is the only museum housed in the original factory, constructed between about 1910 and 1915, that made carousels. The combination of historical information and functioning historic amusement rides is one of my favorite things about the museum. This is because it makes the museum a fun place for all ages! The museum possesses an Allan Herschell 1916 Special #1 Carousel, which provides rides for visitors of all ages. We also possess the only functioning Wurlitzer perforator in the world. This means we can still create rolls for our band organs, which play along our carousel ride! Most visitors do not know that North Tonawanda was home to four amusement companies that produced a large share of the American carousel market," says the education director.

Herschell's obituary gave quite a thorough portrayal of his life so the following are excerpts published in the October 5, 1927, *Evening News*, North Tonawanda: "'Allan Herschell, Pioneer Business Man, Is Dead.' Allan Herschell, 76 years old, died yesterday at his home 97 Elmwood Park. He had been in failing health for some time. Mr. Herschell was directly responsible for the origination of the merry-go-round and other amusement devices.

"Herschell was born in Arlbreath, Forfarshire, Scotland, came to America and located at Buffalo in 1870. Two years later he went into partnership with James Armitage operating a machine shop. Their business showed such rapid development that they were induced to come to North Tonawanda a year later and built a factory. The factory burned down in 1876, was rebuilt and burned down again. After the fires Allan brought in his brother George and organized the Armitage-Herschell company but soon after retired due to ill health and went to New York City for six years. Upon his return to North Tonawanda he induced Armitage-Herschell to make his newly invented merry-go-round which sold very well.

"The manufacture of the merry-go-round was indirectly responsible for the presence of the Wurlitzer Manufacturing company's mammoth plant in North Tonawanda. Armitage-Herschell needed organs made in Germany for their merry-go-rounds. In order to avoid the tariff on the organs they decided to establish a barrel organ in North Tonawanda. Eugene von Kleist was persuaded to come here from Germany and made the necessary organs.

"Armitage-Herschell went out of business in 1902 and was succeeded by Herschell-Spillman. Allan retired from Herschell-Spillman in 1911 and organized the Allan Herschell Company which he retired from in 1923. Allan was survived by his wife Ida M. (Spillman) and a son and daughter."

The Allan Herschell Company specialized in producing portable machines that could be used by traveling carnival operators. The company produced over three thousand hand-carved wooden carousels and outproduced all of its rivals in the carousel industry. Each hand-carved wooden carousel featured striking yet simple horses.

Over the years the Allan Herschell Company expanded its line of amusement park rides and pioneered such concepts as "Kiddieland," a specialized group of rides designed for small children. It also introduced adult thrill rides such as the Twister, the Hurricane, and the Sky Wheel, a double Ferris wheel nearly ninety feet tall. Much of this growth occurred under the ownership of John Wendler and his family starting in the 1930s. The company moved to Buffalo in the late 1950s then was sold to Chance Manufacturing of Wichita, Kansas, a rival maker of amusement rides, in the early 1970s.

Areas to visit in the museum include the Jeanette E. Jones Children's Gallery, which was the original machine shop and now houses the Kiddie Carrousel and other interactive activities for families; the Carving Floor, where volunteer woodcarvers work; and the Wurlitzer Music Roll Department, where the production of paper music rolls takes place using ninety-plus-year-old machines, the only public display of equipment of this type in the country.

Lockport Cave & Underground Boat Ride
5 Gooding St., Lockport; (716) 438-0174; lockportcave.com; open year-round; admission charged

Take a tour and boat ride in the excavation caves used during the construction of the Erie Canal.

"Our tour is a guided historic tour. The cave and pertinent structures utilized water (being bypassed around the locks) for mechanical power by three manufacturing establishments. We are the industrial revolution in America. A few of the 'wow' factors are the underground boat ride, the Gate House when the lights are turned

on ahead in the tunnel, and when people understand the industrialism of those who invented and constructed this large complex," says one of the co-owners.

Begin your visit with the walking tour, where you will explore the historic "Flight of Five" Erie Canal Locks 67 to 71, constructed in 1838, and Locks 34 and 35, which allow boats to travel "uphill" sixty feet through the Niagara Escarpment ridge of rock. During the walk you will see stalactites, flowstone, various geological formations, and artifacts such as drill holes and blasting posts left behind by the workmen who built the tunnel and factories. Next enjoy the one-of-a-kind and mysterious underground boat ride, one of the longest in America. Finally, walk through a 2,100-foot water power tunnel blasted out of solid rock. The Hydraulic Tunnel, which supplied water power to several industries, was the invention of Birdsill Holly.

During your visit you will learn about Birdsill Holly (1822–1894), hydraulic engineer and inventor; Holly Manufacturing Company (1858–1916); Richmond Manufacturing Company (1881–1955); Lockport Pulp Company (1880–1941); and Lockport Hydraulic Company (1856–1907). There are objects on display from all of these industrial plants.

Birdsill Holly was born in Auburn, New York, and when not even a teenager he apprenticed as a general mechanic and millwright in Seneca Falls. In 1855 he invented the Silsby steam fire engine, and in 1858 he founded Holly Manufacturing Company in Lockport. He founded the Holly Steam Combination Company in

1877, which became the American District Steam Company in 1880. Between 1876 and 1888 Holly was awarded 150 patents, second only to Thomas Edison's 1,093 patents. Edison once asked Holly to become his assistant, which Holly refused, but they remained friends. He was married twice and had nine children.

Lockport Cave also offers some seasonal haunted and ghost tours.

Cobblestone Museum
14389 Ridge Rd. W., Albion; (585) 589-9013; cobblestonemuseum.org; open year-round; admission charged

The Cobblestone Museum has three cobblestone buildings built in the early 1800s: the Cobblestone Universalist Church (1834), a parsonage or ward house (ca. 1840), and a schoolhouse (1849). Each building demonstrates a different aspect of pioneer community life.

The Universalist Church was built in the Federal style. The congregation used the church from 1834 to 1865, then came back to life in 1874 until 1895 when a new church was built. It had minimal use until 1960 when the Cobblestone Society was formed and purchased the building. The parsonage was also built in the Federal style and used as a residence until 1975. The District No. 5 Schoolhouse was built in the Greek Revival style with ten-inch-thick walls. Students/scholars were taught here until 1952.

The three cobblestone buildings collectively are designated the Cobblestone National Historic Landmark District. Between 1820 and 1860, approximately one thousand cobblestone buildings were built. Nine hundred were built in NYS, and seven hundred are within an hour's drive of Rochester, New York, the epicenter. Architecture employing cobblestone masonry is truly an Upstate New York phenomenon.

In terms of unique artifacts, the museum has many. "On a macabre note, we have a mid-1800s (before embalming) body cooler that allowed a mortician to show a body in a home for a few days by surrounding the body with ice that slowly melted. The face was visible through a glass-covered door that allowed visitors to see the deceased's face. The exterior looks like a typical 1800s wood coffin and the interior has a full-body metal enclosure that when filled with ice would chill the body. We have one of the first works of famed taxidermist Carl Akeley. It's a stunningly realistic diorama of a vixen fox in its natural habitat. In the 'build a better mousetrap' genre, we have several examples of ways pioneers handled their pest problems. Some are pretty humane compared to the typical snap trap. For 'necessity is the mother of invention,' we have several different butter churns that tried to lighten the load for the pioneer homemaker. One could be rocked like a cradle, and another employed a dog to chase a treat that turned a wheel that would raise and lower the churn handle," says the director.

The complex also has four wood structures that contain artifacts relating to the history and development of agriculture and skilled trades in western New York. The Farmer's Hall gives visitors the opportunity to see rare and unique agricultural tools and implements used throughout the area. The Print Shop, Harness Shop, and Blacksmith Shop are all reminiscent of the working environment of the late nineteenth-century skilled tradesman. From end to end the complex is about a quarter mile long.

Medina Railroad Museum
530 West Ave., Medina; (585) 798-6106; medinarailroadmuseum.org; open year-round; admission charged

The Medina Railroad Museum houses the largest HO Scale model train layout in western New York, and one of the largest in the country. The interactive display, which measures 204 by 14 feet, fittingly resides in a New York Central Railroad freight depot built in 1905 and used as such until 1963.

Their HO Scale layout, which began in 2001, displays how transportation of goods in western New York began with the canal in the 1800s and progressed to trains. It features engines from various railroad lines such as the New York Central, Erie, Lackawanna, Pennsylvania, Lehigh Valley, Nickel Plate, Santa Fe, Erie Lackawanna, and others.

Exhibit areas, besides the model train layout, cover railroading, firefighting, military, and local history.

Railroading history, from the late 1800s to the present day, is all around the museum. Display cases along the perimeter of the "layout room" offer different

artifacts pertaining to different railroad jobs, including track maintenance, locomotive operation, and passenger and freight service. One of the main showcases is dedicated to the New York Central "999" locomotive, which broke the world speed record in May 1893 by going 112.5 miles per hour between Batavia and Corfu.

The firefighting displays were created because the founder of the museum, Martin "Marty" Phelps (1941–2017), was a firefighter in Batavia for twenty-five years. They highlight different equipment used by firefighters over the years, from the basic ladder and hose carts to old-style fire extinguishers and gas masks. Throughout the museum there are 484 fire helmets from around NYS.

Military displays are mostly intertwined in the layout and depict different equipment and trains. The largest display in the layout, located in the "Harbor Division," is a naval ship built by a Pearl Harbor survivor.

Local history consists of the building itself and a brief history of the Ole Heinz Pickle Factory. Heinz used this railroad station to import and export goods all over the nation from 1905 until 1937. The building is the second New York Central freight house built in this location and is one of the longest wooden structures built by the New York Central, coming in at 301 feet long by 25 feet wide. The building became inactive in 1963, with the decline of the New York Central, and was sold to the Hickey's Furniture Store, which used it until 1991, when Martin "Marty" Phelps bought it.

Excursions take place several times during the year in vintage locomotives and train cars made from 1947 to 1957.

Be prepared to be amazed at the size of the Medina Railroad Museum—it's big.

Attica Prison Preservation Foundation & Museum
668 Exchange St., Attica; (585) 708-4388; open year-round; admission free, donations appreciated

This museum tells the history of one of the nation's most infamous state prisons, which opened in 1931. Attica Prison is still in operation as a maximum security facility of two thousand cells.

Attica Prison was originally slated to be named Wyoming Prison for the county it sits in. NYS decided to build a new prison at the end of Governor Al Smith's term of office in 1928. The contracts for building the prison were awarded in September 1929, about a month after the Great Depression began. Most of the labor force was from the local area, plus about seventy-five prisoners from other NYS prisons. The facility was considered to be the ultimate prison, with thirty-foot walls enclosing fifty-five acres. Franklin D. Roosevelt, the forty-fourth governor of NYS from January 1929 to December 1932, was governor throughout the building process.

The museum is housed in a building that was built as the field office for use during construction of the prison. After the prison was complete, the building served numerous purposes until 2012 when the Attica Prison Preservation Foundation bought it with the help of the Corrections Peace Officers Foundation. It became a museum in 2015.

"My favorite aspect of our site is the location. We are as close to Attica State Prison as one can get without actually committing a felony. The 'wow' factor has to be the reactions we get from people when they get locked in the replica we have of a cell, complete with locking sound as the gate closes. My personal favorite artifacts are the pictures and tools from the building of the prison from 1929 to 1931. In

addition we also have on display the clothes that the inmates put on an officer during the riot that took place in 1971. The surviving hostage then donated them to the museum," says the museum's president.

William Pryor Letchworth Museum
1 Letchworth State Park, Castile; (585) 493-2760 or (585) 493-3600; letchworthparkhistory.com; open May through Oct; admission by donation

The museum sits within Letchworth State Park and chronicles the life of William Pryor Letchworth as well as the history of the Genesee Valley.

William Pryor Letchworth was born May 26, 1823, in Brownville, Jefferson County, New York, to Josiah and Ann (Hance) Letchworth. He settled in Buffalo in 1848 and partnered in business with Samuel and Pascal Pratt, manufacturers of saddlery hardware. Wanting to find refuge from day-to-day business, he bought one thousand acres of land near Portage Falls, built a house, and named his estate Glen Iris (in 1914 his home became the Glen Iris Inn). In April 1867, Letchworth was appointed by Governor Dix to represent the counties of this judicial district on the Board of Charities and retired from Pratt & Letchworth in about 1870. He became president of the State Board of Charities in 1878, and in 1883 he was president of the National Conference of Charities. Glen Iris, before it became a state reservation, was famed for its "council house" and relics of Mary Jemison and other Indian celebrities. The grounds were always open to the public and poor children. Letchworth deeded his estate to NYS in 1907. William Letchworth, who was a bachelor, died December 1, 1910, at his Glen Iris estate and is buried in Forest Lawn Cemetery in Buffalo.

"The museum is a collection of artifacts collected by William Pryor Letchworth, the man who donated the original approximately 1,000 acres that eventually expanded to the present 14,350 acres that comprise Letchworth State Park. As part of the museum complex there are two buildings: a circa mid-1700s Seneca council house and Nancy Jemison's log cabin circa 1800, which was moved to a ridge above the museum along with the gravesite and a statue of Mary Jemison. Nancy Jemison was the daughter of Mary Jemison, known as the 'White Woman of the Genesee.' Many tourists are surprised to learn the story of Mary Jemison, a Native American captive of the French and Indian War from Marsh Creek, Pennsylvania, who came to live in the Genesee Valley of NYS and Mr. Letchworth's connection in preserving her legacy," says the historic site manager.

Perhaps the most unique artifact is the Pike mastodon from Pike, New York, which William Pryor Letchworth obtained for his collection. Another unique artifact is the Moses Van Campen tomahawk, which is connected to the story of the expanding frontier in western New York.

Antique Boat Museum
750 Mary St., Clayton; (315) 686-4104; abm.org; open May through Oct; admission charged

Located in the Thousand Islands on the St. Lawrence River, the Antique Boat Museum (ABM) is the premier freshwater boating museum in North America. The museum's collection includes over 320 unique boats and thousands of related artifacts.

"The Antique Boat Museum is not a static museum, as the 4.5-acre campus comes alive with speedboat rides, a working skiff livery, and educational programs. Visitors have the opportunity to take part in the unique experiences of a speedboat ride through the Ride the River program, a guided walk-through of the 1903 Gilded Age houseboat *La Duchesse*, and a row in a traditional St. Lawrence skiff as well as additional experiences through educational programs and special events, including the longest-running (since 1965) antique boat show in North America. Many people don't realize how big the Antique Boat Museum is and expect only one building. The museum offers six buildings (including *La Duchesse*), and a seventh building, the Don Doebler Collections storage facility, is open to visitors on a limited basis, allowing visitors to see and learn about artifacts not on display on the main campus," says the events and communications coordinator.

An article about their first boat show was published in the August 12, 1965, edition of *Thousand Island Sun*: "One of the most beautiful craft to be displayed at the first annual antique boat show in Clayton on August 19 is the twenty-eight-foot *Idyll Oaks*. Built in 1926, this day cruiser has white cedar sides and a varnished mahogany top. It is owned by Mr. and Mrs. Allan R. Youngs, summer residents of Clayton and joint chairmen of the antique boat show which is being held in conjunction with Old Homeweek." The "Quest for Speed" exhibit showcases the history of boat racing, from the outstanding Gold Cup and Harmsworth Trophy winner, *Dixie II*, to record-setting hydroplanes and modified Packard and Liberty airplane engines. The Miller S. and Adelaide S. Gaffney Gallery explores the many different ways in which boats go with the exhibit "Oar Else!" The exhibit features early Dr. Seuss illustrations from Essomarine (now ExxonMobil) advertisements of the 1930s and 1940s. In Seussian fashion, the illustrations portray familiar Seuss characters moving their boats in a variety of creative ways, helping get children (and adults) thinking about what really is possible when it comes to small-craft propulsion. The Dr. Fred Thomas Gallery exhibits "The St. Lawrence Skiff: Our Indigenous Watercraft," which shows how this special small craft developed here on the river primarily as a fishing vessel and how it came to be much more—from a family's utility boat, to a pleasure craft, to a racing machine! The Pauline Morgan Dodge Gallery examines the evolution of different canoe-building traditions.

Three of the museum's interesting crafts are *La Duchesse*, *Little One II*, and *Wild Goose*.

The 106-foot houseboat *La Duchesse* was built for hotelier George Boldt in 1903 with every creature comfort in mind, and was subsequently owned by Life Saver Candy Company's E. J. Noble, and Andrew McNally III, respectively. Over the course of her life, she has been a guesthouse, country club, summer home, and museum exhibit. Although ABM interprets *La Duchesse* as she was during McNally's ownership, details and items from both Boldt and Noble's ownership can also be seen throughout the houseboat. A 1929 single-step hydroplane, *Little One II* traveled from race to race on a trailer made from a Dodge Brothers car chassis. Built by Cliff S. Hadley, she won the Albany Regatta, President's Cup Regatta, and placed second in the Detroit Regatta in 1929. *Little One II* is exhibited unrestored on her original trailer as part of the exhibition "Quest for Speed" in the Morgan Building.

Wild Goose's silhouette is familiar to anyone who has seen ABM's logo, as she has been featured in the logo since 1990. Built in 1915 by Hutchinson Brothers in Alexandria Bay, New York, as a high-speed launch for island commuting and originally named *Onondaga III*, *Wild Goose* was used to ferry visitors to and from Frederick Lovejoy's home on Wellesley Island. In 1928, she was bought by Cleveland E. Dodge of Grindstone Island and renamed *Wild Goose*. The Dodge family used her

Photo: Jim Scherzi

as a family launch for more than seventy years before donating *Wild Goose* to the Antique Boat Museum in 2001.

Jefferson County Historical Society
228 Washington St., Watertown; (315) 782-3491; jeffersoncountyhistory.org; open year-round; admission charged

The Jefferson County Historical Society Museum is housed in the Paddock Mansion, which was built between 1876 and 1878 for Edwin L. and Olive (Wheeler) Paddock. Exhibits reflect the Paddock family and Jefferson County history.

The home was designed by architect John Hose in the Eastlake tradition, which combined Tuscan villa elements "for him" and Swiss chalet "for her." Olive Paddock bequeathed the home to the Society in 1922, and it opened as a museum in 1924.

Edwin L. Paddock (1824–1909) was the son of Loveland and Sophia A. (Foster) Paddock. He married Olive Amelia Wheeler (1835–1922) in 1853. His father established the Black River Bank, often called the Paddock Bank, in 1844. The Black River Bank became the First National Bank of Watertown in 1868, and Edwin became president of the bank when his father died in 1872. Eight years later, in 1880, the bank voluntarily liquidated. Besides banking Paddock also invested in real estate and was worth quite a bit of money at his death. Paddock listed his occupation as "capitalist" in his 1888 passport application.

Exhibits are spread out through three floors and three outbuildings. The Paddock parlor, library and galleries are all located on the first floor of the Paddock Mansion. The sub-floor features the "Comparison Kitchen," "Parlor Stove," "Homespun," and "Kinne Waterwheel" exhibits. The collection of Clarence E. Kinne (1869–1950) is believed to be the largest of its kind anywhere, and has been designated a National Landmark by the American Association of Mechanical Engineers. The second floor features the "Watertown," "Military," "Victorian Pastimes," and "Victorian Lifestyles" exhibits. Outdoor spaces, open in summer, include the early American barn, pioneer cabin, and one-room schoolhouse.

The Society maintains a collection of over one hundred thousand artifacts, including letters, portraits, photographs, American Indian artifacts, militaria, textiles, clothing, farm implements, furniture, and even automobiles! Collections include Victorian costumes once owned by Emma Flower Taylor, the Tyler Coverlet Collection, Paddock estate furniture, over fifteen thousand Huested glass plate negatives from the Huested Photography Studio, the Johnston Studio negatives collection, the Theodore Gégoux Collection, and a large number of GAR and Civil War-related artifacts.

"Some visitors, even lifelong Jefferson County residents, don't realize that many common items were invented here in Jefferson County. Among them are the safety pin, bedsprings, chloroform, the portable steam engine, the Hitchcock lamp, and the paper bag manufacturing machine. On our grounds is also the Hart Massey House, which is believed to be the first frame house in this community, erected possibly as early as 1802 or 1803," says the interim executive director.

Fort Ontario State Historic Site
1 E. Fourth St., Oswego; (315) 343-4711; parks.ny.gov; open May to Columbus Day; admission charged

If you were a bird looking down at Fort Ontario, you would see walls that form a version of a five-pointed star. The existing fort was built in 1839 by the United States and faced with stone masonry beginning in the Civil War. The remains of three earlier fortifications are contained within the earth and timber walls.

At the entrance to each point of the star is a building constructed between 1842 and 1844 with a particular purpose. There are two officers' quarters, the powder magazine, enlisted men's barracks, and a storehouse, which also included a jail. In the center of the star is the parade grounds. One of the officers' quarters contained two six-room apartments for officers, their families, and servants. On the first floor, the front rooms were dining rooms and the rear rooms were kitchens. On the second floor, the front rooms were parlors and the rear rooms were bedrooms. The third floor was occupied by the servants.

"Fort Ontario played a role in nearly every war in American history, from the French and Indian War to the global war on terrorism. The fort's long-term strategic significance and ability to adapt to the military's changing strategic needs, from an outpost of the British Empire to a twenty-first-century US Army Reserve training center, is incredible," says the historic site manager.

One of the most unique artifacts on exhibit is a section of the barbed-wire and chain-link fence that surrounded Fort Ontario in World War II when it served as the only camp or shelter in the United States for Holocaust refugees, established by executive order of President Franklin D. Roosevelt. It is iconic because it symbolizes where, on August 5, 1944, everyday Americans and the national press first met Holocaust victims and learned their personal stories of persecution and survival at the hands of the Nazis, which resulted in Holocaust stories moving from the back to the front pages of US newspapers. Another section of fence is on display in the Fort Ontario Emergency Refugee Shelter Gallery, in the landmark "Americans and the Holocaust" exhibit that opened in 2018. First-time visitors are surprised to learn of the fort's unique history as the only US camp for Holocaust refugees during World War II, and that the Fort Ontario refugees were the first to be granted asylum in the United States, opening doors for later groups following post–World War II refugee legislation.

President Franklin D. Roosevelt (1882–1945) asked his Secretary of the Interior to send someone to Italy to bring nearly 1,000 refugees to America; that someone was Special Assistant Ruth Gruber. The 982 chosen ones were hand-picked following a certain criteria. Gruber chose families and survivors with skills to run a camp and those who had escaped concentration camps. It was made very clear to the refugees that they were coming as visitors until the war ended and would not be garnering American citizenship. The group took the two-week journey to America on the USS *Henry Gibbins* troop transport ship along with wounded American soldiers. One of the young voyagers tried Jell-O and chewing gum for the first time in her life. All were happy to see the Statue of Liberty but not happy to be loaded on trains, similar to trains that brought fellow countryman to concentration camps, and see barbed-wire fencing around the camp. They were not totally free, but they were not in prison.

Another favorite is the bloodstained shelter half (tent) of Captain Lewis B. Porter, 81st New York Infantry Regiment. His bloodstained shirt with the missing sleeve where his arm was amputated after being wounded at the Battle of Chaffin's Farm, and a letter to his wife written for him by a hospital steward predicting his full recovery, are the most compelling artifacts on exhibit. These were sent home to his widow in Oswego after Porter died of blood poisoning and symbolize the enormous human cost of the American Civil War and the struggle to end slavery in the United States.

H. Lee White Marine Museum
1 W. First St., Oswego; (315) 342-0480; hlwmm.org; open year-round; admission charged

This museum, overlooking Oswego Harbor, offers hundreds of years of maritime history—and you can even climb up the Oswego West Pierhead Lighthouse, situated within Oswego's Historic Maritime District.

The museum was named after Harris Lee White (1912–1969), who was an attorney, served in the US Navy during World War II, was appointed assistant secretary of the Air Force by President Eisenhower in 1953, and was the head of the second-largest fleet of commercial cargo vessels in the world at the time of his death. The museum was founded in 1982 under the auspices of the Port of Oswego Authority and led by Mrs. Rosemary Nesbitt (1924–2009), a former SUNY Oswego theater professor and City of Oswego historian.

The museum's main facility formerly was the Port of Oswego Authority offices, quarters, workshop, and powerhouse for the one-million-bushel grain elevator located on the West First Street Pier. Built in 1925 to capitalize on grain shipments on the Lake Ontario–St. Lawrence River commercial route, the elevator functioned until the 1990s and was demolished in 1998.

The museum's extensive collection includes Native American artifacts such as a 350-year-old dugout canoe that was discovered locally, the original Fresnel lens from the Oswego Lighthouse, shipbuilding tools, maritime artwork, shipwreck artifacts, and boat models.

Outside the museum building are three vessels. You can tour the *LT-5* and *Boat 8* and view the *Eleanor D*. The USAT LT-5 is a rare World War II–era tugboat that participated in the D-Day invasion in 1944 and even shot down a German plane. It was christened the *Major Elisha K. Henson* and was launched on November 22, 1943. After the war the tugboat, now a National Historic Landmark, was used on the Great Lakes. The 1927 NYS *Derrick Boat 8* is listed on the National Register of Historic Places. It was built by the Department of Waterways' Department Forces and used to maintain the NYS Barge Canal between 1927 and 1984. *Eleanor D.*, the last American commercial fishing vessel on Lake Ontario, was built in Erie, Pennsylvania, in 1948 and purchased by William Cahill Sr. and William Cahill Jr. of Oswego, New York, in 1958. The forty-ton vessel has a hull built from surplus World War II steel sheeting; has a five-foot draft, twelve-foot beam, and forty-two-foot length; and has endured the twenty-five-foot swells not uncommon to Lake Ontario. The Cahill family used it until 1979.

A short boat ride is involved in visiting the Oswego West Pierhead Lighthouse, built in 1934 to improve upon and replace the existing lights of Oswego Harbor. The lighthouse lantern was automated in 1969, which ending the era of light-keeping as a profession in Oswego, and the original fourth order Fresnel Lens was removed and placed in the care of the H. Lee White Marine Museum in 1995. Oswego West Pierhead Lighthouse is still a component utilized by seafaring vessels on Lake Ontario.

Frederic Remington Art Museum
303 Washington St., Ogdensburg; (315) 393-2425; fredericremington.org; open year-round; admission charged

This museum houses a comprehensive collection of original Remington paintings, sketches, and sculptures, as well as a broad array of personal effects and correspondence. Visitors often ask if Remington lived here, and the answer is no, but he was from the area and his wife lived here after his death.

Frederic Sackrider Remington (1861–1909) married Eva Caten (1859–1918) in 1884 in Gloversville, New York. They spent the first year of their marriage in Kansas City, then lived in New Rochelle, New York, and Ridgefield, Connecticut, and often vacationed in Upstate New York and out to western states in the summer. Eva took up residence in Ogdensburg in about 1915 and bequeathed Frederic's art collection to the town, provided there was a suitable place for it to be protected. Frederic's collection was first stored in the Ogdensburg Public Library, and even survived a fire that burned the library down in 1921 because the collection was in the library vault. Frederic's work next went to a house built in 1810 by David Parish, which became this museum in 1923.

The great majority of items came directly from Eva Remington's 1918 estate. They include sketchbooks, endless pages of notes, photographs—even the cigars that were in Frederic's pocket before he died. The museum's collection includes a full spectrum of the artist's work, including some of his earliest achievements, many published paintings and drawings, and an inspiring variety of late-life paintings, which focus on the landscape. The collection of Remington's paintings, drawings, and bronzes is, of course, the most important thing in the museum, but it's the combination of all the elements that lets you imagine Frederic Remington here, perhaps smoking cigars and drinking whiskey into the night with any member of his circle of friends.

"My favorite aspect of the Frederic Remington Art Museum is the comprehensive, extraordinary collection of original art by Frederic Remington and a new permanent exhibit of the art of Remington's colleague, who was also raised in Ogdensburg, Sally James Farnham. Many folks now, with the proliferation of Remington sculpture reproductions, only know the artist as a sculptor and are amazed at the quality and diversity of his paintings and drawings on display," says the director.

St. Lawrence Power and Equipment Museum
1755 State Hwy. 345, Madrid; (315) 323-5349; slpowermuseum.com; open May through Oct; admission free, donations appreciated, admission for shows

This is not just a museum; it is a living-history mini village that focuses on power systems, equipment, and related knowledge of the nineteenth and early twentieth centuries in the North Country.

"We feel that one unique thing about our museum is that most artifacts and displays are able to be put to use, rather than simply displayed. Most commonly this is done during our two exhibitions each year when museum members and volunteers actually use many of the items on hand at the museum as well as bring many from their personal collections. This includes activities such as crop field preparation and planting, corn binding and chopping, oat threshing, sawing lumber at the sawmill, making shingles, blacksmith shop operating, antique tractor pulling, horse pulling, tractor parades, and gas, diesel, and steam engines operating, all in addition to the more static displays. Unique artifacts include our operating steam engine; the Harden collection, which is an extensive collection of horse-drawn equipment from the Harden family, housed in our over five-thousand-square-foot Carriage Barn; the new Fort Tribute, a Civil War–era interpretive center; and an 1850s schoolhouse. Visitors are often amazed at the depth of the collection. There is truly something for everyone due to the variety of displays. While all are centered around early to mid-twentieth-century life, there is something for those interested in agricultural history, education, transportation, textiles, lumber-making, and even military history," says the president of the board of trustees.

Some of the equipment on display includes a road roller, Bay City excavator power shovel, A. B. Farquhar steam engine built in 1922, a log splitter, a Lane sawmill built in 1920, a shingle mill, small engines, and a vertical sawmill.

Buildings in the complex include Heritage Fibers, Equine Pavillion, Collections Building, and Schoolhouse No. 12. The Heritage Fibers building might be offering demonstrations on rug hooking, spinning, weaving on a frame loom, tatting, quilting, and rug braiding. The Equine Pavillion offers assorted horse-related programs. The Collections Building has displays of early labor-saving devices, including a hand-operated corn sheller, vegetable choppers and slicers, a washing machine, and even a bone grinder to provide calcium for egg layers. The schoolhouse was originally from the town of LeRoy and in use until 1915, then moved in 1990 and moved again to the museum in 2011.

Additional exhibit areas include the Goolden-Mann World War II farmstead original to the museum complex; the 1890 Walker Farm Granary; an early 1900s-style maple sugar house; the Curtis family windmill circa 1900; a log cabin circa 1832, originally from Lisbon, New York; a cobbler shop with tools left behind by the owner, who retired in 1950; the Antique Tractor Building, the Paul E. Merrill Horse-Drawn Equipment Building; and a reproduction of a 1927–1928 Texaco gas station in Madrid, New York.

A lot of volunteer labor went into creating this thirteen-acre campus of life in the olden days in the St. Lawrence River region.

Thematic Index

Local History & Genealogy

Military History

Nature & Natural History

New York State Industries

Political History & Homes

Sports

Antique Boat Museum, 195–197
International Motor Racing Research Center, 121–122
Lake Placid Olympic Museum, 7–8
National Soaring Museum, 103–105
Northeast Classic Car Museum, 68–69

Transportation

Antique Boat Museum, 195–197
Dunkirk Lighthouse & Veterans Park Museum, 94–95
Empire State Aerosciences Museum, 42–43
Erie Canal Cruises, 21–22
Erie Canal Museum, 114–115
Fire Island Lighthouse Preservation Society, 163–165
H. Lee White Marine Museum, 200–202
Hudson River Maritime Museum, 59–61
Lockport Cave & Underground Boat Ride, 188–190
Medina Railroad Museum, 191–192
National Soaring Museum, 103–105
New York Transit Museum, 170–172
Northeast Classic Car Museum, 68–69
Trolley Museum of New York, 61–62
USS *Slater* Destroyer Escort Historical Museum, 33–34
Walter Elwood Museum of the Mohawk Valley and ALCO Historical & Technical
    Society, 71–73

Women's History

The Alice T. Miner Museum, 1–2
Susan B. Anthony Museum & House, 111–112
Women's Rights National Historical Park, 124–125

Photo Credits

Courtesy of the Alice T. Miner Colonial Collection/by Paul Frederick 2; Copyright Fort Ticonderoga/by Carl Heilman II 4; Courtesy of Karen McLaughlin Cuccinello 5, 13, 14, 15, 16, 23, 24, 25, 31, 32, 37, 38, 39, 40, 44, 45, 49, 59, 60, 62, 64, 67, 70, 72, 74, 83, 87, 93, 103, 106, 107, 111, 131; Courtesy of Franklin County Historical Museum Society 9, 10; Courtesy of Wilder House, photo by Rick Auger 11; Courtesy of Adirondack Experience, Museum at Blue Mountain Lake 17, 18; Courtesy of Piseco Lake Historical Society 19, 20; Courtesy of Connie McLaughlin 21; Courtesy of Constable Hal 27; Courtesy of Chapman Historical Museum 29; Courtesy of Warrensburgh Museum 30; Courtesy of USS Slater Destroyer Escort Historical Museum 33; Courtesy of Hart Cluett Museum of Historic Rensselaer County 35, 36; Courtesy of Saratoga National Historic Park 41; Courtesy of Skene Manor, photo's by Sally Ann Raino 46, 47; Courtesy of Delaware County Historical Association & Museum 50; Courtesy of Hanford Mills Museum 51; Courtesy of the Bronck Museum, Greene County Historical Society 53; Courtesy of Thomas Cole National Historic Site, photo by Escape Brooklyn 54 & photo by Peter Aaron Otto 55; Courtesy of Bethel Woods Center for the Arts 56, 57; Courtesy of Time and the Valleys Museum 58; Courtesy of Roberson Museum 65; Courtesy of Northeast Classic Car Museum 69; Courtesy of Oneida Community Mansion House 75, 76; Courtesy of H.P. Sears Oil Co. Museum 78; Courtesy of Oneida County History Center 80; Courtesy of Hyde Hall, photos by Joe Maney 81, 82; Courtesy of Bobbi Ryan 85; Courtesy of Patrick Cullen American Museum of Cutlery 89, 90; Courtesy of Seneca-Iroquois National Museum 92; Courtesy of Dunkirk Lighthouse 95; Courtesy of Alfred Ceramic Art Museum 96; Courtesy of Pioneer Oil Museum 98; Courtesy of Seward House Historic Museum 100; Courtesy of Ward W. O'Hara Agricultural & Country Living Museum 101; Courtesy of National Soaring Museum & Harris Hill Soaring Corp. 104; Courtesy of National Warplane Museum/Jamieson R. Steele 109; Courtesy of George Eastman House 113; Courtesy of Erie Canal Museum 114; From the collection of The Stickley Museum, L & JG Stickley Inc. 116; Courtesy of Ontario County Historical Museum 117; Courtesy Phelps Community Historical Society 118; Courtesy of Schuyler County Historical Society 120; Courtesy of International Motor Racing Research Center 122; Courtesy National Memorial Day Museum & Historical Society 123; Courtesy of public domain 125; Courtesy of The Corning Museum of Glass 126; Courtesy of Bully Hill Museum 127: Courtesy of Waverly Museum 129; Courtesy of Museum of the Earth 132; Courtesy History Center in Tompkins County 134; Courtesy Hoffman Clock Museum 135; Courtesy of Hotchkiss Peppermint Museum 137; Courtesy of Dundee Area Historical Society 138; Courtesy of Yates County History Center 140; Courtesy of FASNY Museum of Firefighting, copyrighted by the museum 142; Courtesy of Olana, photo by Peter Aaron 143; Courtesy of Locust Grove Estate, photo by Nathaniel Cooper 145; Courtesy of NPS/Vanderbilt Mansion 147; Courtesy of Museum Village at Old Smith's Clove 148; Courtesy of Boscobel House and Gardens, photo by Lauren Daisley 151; Courtesy of Putnam History Museum, photo by Cassie Ward 152; Courtesy of The New Castle Historical Society 155, 156; Courtesy of Washington Irving's Sunnyside 158; Courtesy of Old Bethpage Village Restoration, photos by Carol Beckerman 159, 160; Enn Li Photography/Getty Images 162, 163; Vicki Jauron, Babylon and Beyond Photography/Getty Images 164; Courtesy of Brenna McCormick-Thompson/The Whaling Museum & Education Center 165, 166; Courtesy Bronx Historical Society 168; Courtesy of Old Stone House of Brooklyn 169; Photos by Black Paw Photo/New York Transit Museum 170, 171; Photo by Dimitri Maisuradze and Zurab Qatamadze/Museum of Jewish Heritage 172; Courtesy of National 9/11 Memorial & Museum 174; Library of Congress 176; Barry Winiker/Getty Images 178; Courtesy of The Jacques Marchais Museum of Tibetan Art 180; Courtesy of Frank Lloyd Wright's Martin House 181; Courtesy of Theodore Roosevelt Inaugural Site 183; Courtesy of Lynne Belluscio/LeRoy Historical Society 186; Courtesy of Lockport Cave & Underground Boat Ride 189; Courtesy of Medina Railroad Museum 191, 192; Courtesy of Attica Prison Preservation Foundation & Museum 193; Courtesy of Jim Scherzi/Antique Boat Museum 196; Courtesy of Jefferson County Historical Society 197; Courtesy of Fort Ontario State Historic Site 199; Courtesy of H. Lee White Marine Museum 201 and Courtesy of St. Lawrence Power and Equipment Museum 204.

Acknowledgments

The following people and organizations helped enhance information or sent photographs for the following sites via email, phone, or on-site visits.

The 1890 House Museum—Associate director Rosalie D. Hopko

Alfred Ceramic Art Museum—Operations and programs manager Bill Giese and director and chief curator Wayne Higby

The Alice T. Miner Museum—Director Ellen Adams

The Almanzo Wilder Homestead—Board member Karen Carre

American Museum of Cutlery—Founder Patrick J. Cullen

Antique Boat Museum—Events and communications coordinator Caitlin Playle and executive director Rebecca Hopfinger

Attica Prison Preservation Foundation & Museum—President Patrick Gallaway

Battle of Plattsburgh Association—President Keith A. Herkalo

Boscobel House and Gardens—Director of communications Lauren Daisley and director and curator Jennifer Catlquist

Bronck Museum and Library—Curator Shelby Mattice and operations manager Jennifer Barnhart

Bronx County Historical Society—Librarian/archivist Steven Payne PhD

Bully Hill Vineyard Museum—Director of marketing Sean King

Central New York Living History Center—Executive director Cindy Stoker

Chapman Historical Museum—Executive director Tim Weidner

Chenango County Historical Society Museum and Campus—Executive director Jessica Moquin

Cobblestone Museum—Director Doug Farley

Constable Hall—Trustee Peter Hayes

The Corning Museum of Glass—Manager of public relations and special media projects Kim Thompson

Delaware County Historical Association & Museum—Director Tim Duerden

Dunkirk Lighthouse—Events coordinator and treasurer of the lighthouse board David Briska

Erie Canal Cruises—Marketing director John Costanzo

Erie Canal Museum—Director of communications and outreach Vicki Krisak

FASNY Museum of Firefighting—Collections manager Christina Lillpopp

Fort Klock Historic Restoration—Tour guide Les Bearclaw Stewart

Fort Ontario State Historic Site—Historic site manager Paul Lear

Fort Ticonderoga—Group tour and communications coordinator Ryann Wiktorko

Frank Lloyd Wright's Martin House—Marketing manager Suzanne Badgley

Franklin County Historical & Museum Society—Volunteers Carol Poole and Phyllis Carley

Frederic Remington Art Museum—Director Laura A. Foster

Fulton County Museum—Executive director Samantha Hall-Saladino

George Eastman House—Curator of George Eastman Legacy Collection Kathy Connor

H. Lee White Marine Museum—Curator Michael R. Pittavino

Hanford Mills Museum—Executive director Liz Callahan

Hart Cluett Museum—Executive director Karin Krasevac-Lenz and curator/archivist Stacey Draper

Haverstraw Brick Museum—Brick Museum staff

Herschell Carrousel Factory Museum—Education director Ian K. Seppala

The History Center in Tompkins County—Director of archives and research services Donna Eschenbrenner

Hoffman Clock Museum—Assistant curator Dave Richardson

Holland Land Office Museum—Executive director Ryan J. Duffy

Hotchkiss Peppermint Museum—Director Patricia Alena, aka "Peppermint Patty"

Howe House Museum—Director Diane J. Goodman

H.P. Sears Oil Co. Inc. Service Station Museum—Volunteer manager Pat Corbett

Hudson River Maritime Museum—Executive director Lisa Cline

Hyde Hall—Former long-term board member Robert Schenider and marketing and publicity manager John Aborn

International Maple Museum Centre—Acting board of directors president Don Moser

International Motor Racing Research Center—Visitor services/outreach coordinator Kip Zeiter

The Jacques Marchais Museum of Tibetan Art—Marketing and public programs manager Frank Saulle

Jefferson County Historical Society—Interim executive director Toni Engleman

Johnson Hall State Historic Site—Tour guide Audrey Humphrey

Knickerbocker Mansion—Docent Leslie Allen

Lake Placid Olympic Museum—Director Alison Haas

LeRoy House and Jell-O Gallery—Director Lynne Belluscio

Livingston County Historical Society Museum—Museum administrator Anna Kowalchuk

Lockport Cave & Underground Boat Ride—Co-owner Tom Callahan

Locust Grove Estate—Executive director Kenneth F. Snodgrass

Mabee Farm Historic Site—Educator/tour guide Michael Diana

Madison County Historical Society, Cottage Lawn Museum—Director Sydney Lotus and docent Terri Philips

Medina Railroad Museum—Group sales and volunteer coordinator Caitlyn Klotzbach

Museum at Bethel Woods Center for the Arts—Assistant curator Julia Fell

Museum Village at Old Smith's Clove—Director of marketing Martina Dryer

The National Memorial Day Museum—Executive director Cyndi Park-Sheils

National Soaring Museum—Director Traff Doherty and administrative assistant Jean Doherty

National Warplane Museum—Volunteer who wears many hats, Jamieson R. Steele.

New Castle Historical Society—Executive director Jennifer Plick

New York State Military Museum and Veterans Research Center—Librarian/archivist Jim Gandy and assistant curator Christopher Morton

New York Transit Museum—Director Concetta Bencivenga and press and marketing strategist Chelsea Newburg

Northeast Classic Car Museum—Operations assistant Jake DeRochie

Olana State Historic Site—Director Amy Hausmann; presidents of The Olana Partnership Sean Sawyer and Washburn and Susan Oberwager, and director of advancement and marketing Melanie Hasbrook

Old Bethpage Village Restoration—Village manager Timothy Van Wickler

Old Stone House—Executive director Kim Maier

Old Westbury Gardens—Senior account executive Christine Sammarco

Oneida Community Mansion House—Executive director Christine Hall O'Neil

Oneida County Historical Society—Director of education and outreach
Rebecca McLain

Ontario County Historical Museum—Executive director Edward Varno

Paleontological Research Institution at Museum of the Earth & Cayuga Nature Center—
Manager of marketing and communications Jim Harper

Phelps Mansion Museum—House manager and my tour guide Joe Schuerch

Pioneer Oil Museum of New York—Board member Kelly Lounsberry

Piseco Lake Historical Society—President Frederick Adcock and vice president Cynthia Adcock

Putnam History Museum—Executive director Cassie Ward

Roberson Museum and Science Center—Executive director Michael Grasso

Russian History Foundation—Seminary student David, originally from Sweden

St. Lawrence Power and Equipment Museum—Board of trustees president
Ron Sheppard and secretary Roger S. Austin

Saratoga National Historical Park—Park ranger and historian Eric Schnitzer

Schuyler County Historical Society—Executive director Glenda Gephart

Seneca-Iroquois National Museum—Director Joe Stahlman and inventory manager Jeremy Jones

Seward House Historic Museum—Executive director Billye Chabot

Skene Manor—President Richard F. Brewer

Slate Valley Museum—Interim director Sarah Kijowski

Stickley Museum—Director Amanda L. Clifford

Swart–Wilcox House Museum—Program chair (and one of the chief cook and bottle washers)
Helen Rees

Theodore Roosevelt Inaugural Site—Executive director Stanton H. Hudson and development
and communications manager Lindsey Visser

Thomas Cole National Historic Site—Executive director Elizabeth B. Jacks

Time and the Valleys Museum—Director Donna Steffens

Tioga History Museum—Executive assistant Jacob Evanek

Trolley Museum of New York—President Erik Garces

USS Slater Destroyer Escort Museum—Visitor engagement and program manager Shanna
Schuster

Vanderbilt Mansion—Acting chief of interpretation Allan Dailey

The Vander-Ende Onderdonk House—Board of directors member Linda Monte

Walter Elwood Museum of the Mohawk Valley—Executive director Ann M. Peconie and office
assistant Chastity George

Ward W. O'Hara Agricultural & Country Living Museum—Museum aide
Rob Norton and director Tim Quill

Warrensburgh Museum of Local History—Director Steve Parisi

Washington Irving's Sunnyside—Marketing associate Kerry Erlanger

Washington's Headquarters State Historic Site—Historic site manager
Elyse B. Goldberg

Waverly Museum—Board member and curator Barbara Koehn

The Whaling Museum & Education Center—Curator of education
Brenna McCormick-Thompson

William Pryor Letchworth Museum—Historic site manager Brian Scriven

Yates County History Center—Administrative assistant Lisa Harper

About the Author

Karen McLaughlin Cuccinello grew up in Putnam/Westchester County, New York, then moved to the little rural town of Summit, Schoharie County, New York, in 1978, where she still resides. She is a self-published author of numerous Schoharie County and northern Delaware County historical books and articles (books are on Amazon.com), genealogist for over thirty years, Town of Summit and Village of Stamford historian, weekly Summit columnist for a Cobleskill, New York, newspaper, historian in the Stamford Village Library history room, and deputy director of the Region 7 Association of Public Historians NYS.